The Secret Journals of

Queen Elizabeth II

The Secret Journals of

Queen Elizabeth II

Edited by
Constance, Lady Crabtree

VIRGIN

Copyright © Paul James 1988 and 1990

This edition published in Great Britain in 1990 by
Virgin Books
A division of W. H. Allen & Co Plc
26 Grand Union Centre
338 Ladbroke Grove
London W10 5AH

First published in 1988 by Columbus Books Ltd

Cataloguing in Publication Data available from the British Library

ISBN 0-86369-393-8

Designed by Paperweight

Typeset by Poole Typesetting (Wessex) Limited
Printed and bound by The Bath Press, Avon

Dedicated to Morag Auchtermuchty, my 'wee chum' at Balmoral Castle, and my late husband, Claude. May he rest in peace, until we meet again.

Foreword

I knew instantly from the 'Miss Piggy' expression that Her Majesty was not pleased. At work in her private apartment at Windsor Castle, overlooking the formal gardens of the East Terrace, the Queen's fingers drummed noisily on her desk as she perused an item from one of the many red despatch boxes.

'Just look at this, Constance,' she said, holding up a magazine cutting that had been sent to her by the Australian ambassador.

'QUEEN LIZ THE PENNY-PINCHER,' screamed the headline. 'Not only does Her Majesty go around Buckingham Palace switching off unnecessary lights, but she has now stopped giving the Royal Household breakfast in order to save money. The traditional staff afternoon tea is also alleged to be under threat . . .'

'They make me sound like Scrooge,' she grumbled.

'Yes, Ma'am,' I agreed, sorely tempted to point out how much I missed the bacon and kidneys that we used to have each morning.

'Sometimes I wish I could tell *my* side of the story,' she continued. 'Life doesn't come trimmed with ermine, you know.'

'No, Ma'am.'

It never ceased to amaze me, all the time I was in her service, that Her Majesty could still become irritated by journalistic attacks. There were times when I too wished that she could make her own point of view public, if only to stop her taking all the press comment to heart.

'We can have the second bar of the electric fire on if you're cold, Constance,' she added, thoughtfully.

'No, Ma'am, one bar is quite sufficient.'

The Queen smiled.

A few weeks later I was back on duty again, this time in one of the Buckingham Palace drawing rooms. It was an extremely wet

Tuesday afternoon in mid-July and had been a very average day. Her Majesty had kissed hands twice, held a personal investiture, toured a converted monastery making microchip combustibles for the Ministry of Defence, entertained a trade union leader, an ex-football manager, an aged actress and the chairman of the British Gas Corporation at an informal luncheon, and was now – with one eye on the 3.30 at Newmarket – actively engaged in making notes for the Prime Minister's weekly audience. I was busy adding some discreet touches of extra decoration to a couple of shop-bought almond slices, ready for Her Majesty's consumption in the royal tea tent at a garden party being held later in the day, when suddenly, to my astonishment, the Queen remarked that she would like to publish *the story of her life.*

As I stooped to retrieve half a dozen glacé cherries from the faded Wilton, I urged Her Majesty to consider the implications. I felt it my duty to advise Her Majesty that the idea was pure folly. After all, so *many* people have written biographies already . . . There would never be a market for it, I assured her. No publisher would risk financing yet another life story of the monarch. Realizing that the proposition simply wasn't viable, and certainly couldn't make her any money, the Queen nodded in agreement and returned to the recommendations of the Cork Report. Yet, as I wrestled one of Her Majesty's corgis for the last remaining cherry, I could not help wishing that there were some way in which I could help Her Majesty fulfil this ambition. It would, after all, be the ultimate royal service.

My first dealings with the Queen had not been happy. I had spent two gruelling years at Madame Bernice's Academy of Refinement and Beauty with the ambition of becoming Deb of the Year when Her Majesty saw fit to abolish the whole debutante system and thereby scuppered my chances. Instead, 'informal luncheons' at the Palace were introduced, but small talk over a lamb chop is no substitute for presentation at Court. So disappointed was I that my father said that I could have a coming-out ball when I was 21. My twin sister Millamant and I both wanted our own separate celebrations, but Father insisted that one large ball would be preferable to having two small ones, so eventually we had a huge party at the lovely Assembly Rooms in York. The occasion was to seal my fate.

As I sat looking demure in off-the-shoulder crêpe-de-chine, sipping my very first pink gin, I glanced up and saw a stunning young man across the room. In those days, of course, it wasn't seemly for a young girl to approach a man. Instead I fluttered my eyelashes at him seductively. Sure enough, it wasn't long before Claude Crabtree came over and asked if I'd got something in my eye. I didn't see where the stunning young man went. Claude and I spent the entire evening dancing together and, after a whirlwind romance on the back of his motorbike, we were married at the little church in the gloomy Yorkshire village of Cleghorn St Percy, which has been overlooked for generations by the Crabtree family seat.

Love may be blind, but even I knew that Claude was a difficult and selfish man. When I expressed a desire to see the world he bought me an atlas. I assumed he had misunderstood me, but when he gave me an engagement ring with the tiniest diamond I'd ever seen, declaring that he didn't want the glare to hurt my eyes, I began to realize that wanton extravagance was not one of his many failings. Notwithstanding their family motto, 'Solum Optima Nobis Satis Bona' ('Only the Best is Good Enough for Us'), the Crabtrees are notoriously mean. Claude's father, Lord Montfort Crabtree, took an instant dislike to me. He lived to the ripe old age of 102, and I have always harboured the suspicion that he lingered deliberately just to spite me.

Eventually Lord Montfort popped his clogs, probably realizing that even the Crabtrees are not immortal. Thus my husband became the ninth Baron Crabtree, his ancestor Sir Hector Crabtree having been ennobled by George III in 1780, and I became a Lady. It was thrilling for someone of my background to receive a title, although many a jealous hussy has since implied that I married Claude for his money. Considering his obese and somewhat repellent figure in later life, it was perhaps an easy conclusion for them to draw.

The highlight of my life as a society hostess came in 1969 when Her Majesty the Queen and the Duke of Edinburgh honoured us with their presence at dinner one evening. It was a relatively informal occasion, although I did wear the Crabtree tiara and a string of Mother's pearls. On reflection, I suppose the Queen may have felt a little under-dressed, but if she did she didn't show it. Unfortunately this was at the time when Her Majesty was being trailed by a camera crew for a television special to be called *Royal Family*, and, in a somewhat misguided attempt to show the viewers what ordinary mortals the royal family are, the director insisted that the Queen help me to wash up. We must have washed my Wedgwood dinner service ten times before they got the shots they required.

I was very disappointed when I watched the finished film some months later to see that the cosy scene in my kitchen had ended up on the cutting-room floor. Instead we had shots of Her Majesty tossing a salad at Balmoral. Nevertheless, that evening we had both enjoyed a good giggle and the Queen managed to look radiant even while wrist-deep in soapy water.

Through Claude's position as Chairman of the Swine Breeders' Federation (he had a lifelong penchant for pigs and owned some of the best sties in Yorkshire) I came into contact with royalty on numerous occasions and I think the Queen always noticed the practical side of my nature. When the Duke's hair fell out it was I who suggested that she stuff a pin-cushion with it.

I also discovered that Her Majesty is an extremely caring person. It was she who brought it to my attention that Claude was an inveterate gambler, the Queen Mother having spotted him disappearing into a Slough betting shop on more than one occasion, and she never failed to ask about his rupture whenever they met.

So it was that in 1984, when Claude joined that great pig farm in the sky, I received an unexpected letter from Buckingham Palace asking me if I would take on the position of relief Woman of the Bedchamber to the Queen. I think perhaps Her Majesty had taken pity on me, Claude having failed to pay his insurance premiums since 1963, although nothing was ever said. The job of WoB carries no pay but many perks. The most exciting was the chance it provided to see all the royal homes *from the inside* – not just the state rooms, but the smaller, less formal apartments.

The Queen's Diary Closet at Windsor Castle is a room that few people know about and one I came upon entirely by accident. It was the day after Her Majesty's 60th birthday, on which I fear I may have somewhat over-indulged at the staff celebrations in the Castle cellars. Even Her Majesty looked a bit jaded the next day and remarked that she could well have done without having to entertain King Juan Carlos and Queen Sofia of Spain on their state visit.

'It's only the second visit ever of a Spanish monarch to Britain,' she said, tapping her foot as we awaited their arrival from Heathrow. 'Why did they have to come today?'

She put on one of her glum expressions and failed to smile even when the Duke shouted, 'Keep your chins up, Lilibet!' as their car came into view.

I felt decidedly off-colour all day and excused myself from the state banquet in the evening, to which I had been invited to make up the numbers. Wandering around the York Tower in a desperate attempt to find a bathroom, I found myself in the diary closet by mistake. One side of the room was filled with red leather-bound volumes, diaries that spanned over 40 years, each filled with the Queen's handwriting. I recognized the books immediately because often when I was called upon to take Her Majesty a cup of Horlicks at night I would find her sitting up in bed, bespectacled, scribbling in a red leather book which she always tucked between the winceyette sheets as soon as I entered.

I was filled with excitement. Now I knew where the diaries were kept, I could not resist leafing through a couple of volumes. Here were Her Majesty's thoughts recorded for posterity, night after night, year after year – the reflections, views and observations of the best-known yet least-known woman in the world. I read on and on with wonderment and mounting fascination, guilty at reading such intensely personal documents, yet at the same time thrilled to be holding history in my hands. In orderly succession from 1947 (the year of her marriage) onwards, the journals recorded *everything*, and I noticed that, just as I do, the Queen tucked little notes, letters, press cuttings and memos between the pages of each volume. Here was an apology from Winston Churchill for dropping cigar ash on a priceless carpet, a postcard from Mustique signed 'Margaret' . . . I could not prevent myself from delving into volume after volume.

That night as I lay in my bed I could hear the Queen's words echoing over and over again in my mind: 'Constance, I would love to be able to publish my life story.'

Perhaps it had been wrong of me to advise against it. Maybe I *should* have encouraged her to write her autobiography. And perhaps some publisher somewhere could be persuaded to take the risk. After all, Queen Victoria had published *her* journals ... Suddenly it came to me. My discovery of Queen Elizabeth's own diaries was the answer. Why should the Queen not follow her great-great-great grandmother's example? I knew at once that it was my bounden duty to release them for publication, for posterity. Could it be that my stumbling upon the diaries unexpectedly was *meant to be?* What a wonderful surprise it would be for the Queen to find her own words at last in print. I felt it a great honour to occupy a position whereby I could perform such a service for the Queen of England.

Immediately I set about editing the volumes, selecting extracts from here and there over the forty glorious years. I spent every spare moment closeted with the journals, and though I may have omitted passages of too intimate a nature, not wishing to cause our beloved royal family embarrassment, I hope that the extracts I have chosen will at long last show the Queen as she *really* is.

So many stories are written about royalty, so many of them pure fabrication, yet the Queen can never publicly speak out or reveal her true feelings. I am certain therefore that Her Majesty will be deeply grateful that at long last her opinions and personal attitudes to life can be known by all.

Constance, Lady Crabtree

CRABTREE HALL
CLEGHORN ST PERCY
NORTH YORKSHIRE
14th May 1984

Your Majesty,

I was deeply touched by your great concern at the demise of my dear husband, Claude, earlier this month. Though it may not have been his wish to depart this earth at a dinner party, face downwards in the 'bombe surprise', it was typically inconsiderate of him not to have waited until after the meal. As he embarrassed me in life, so he made a fool of me in death. I was only thankful that the incident did not occur during the Brown Windsor and that no lasting stain was left on my double damask.

Faced now with astronomical death duties, and with more than a few gaps in my social calendar, I was more than grateful to receive your Majesty's generous offer of employment. I look forward very much to taking up my post as relief Woman of the Bedchamber. As commanded, I shall be at the Privy Purse Door of Buckingham Palace first thing on Monday morning, complete with rubber gloves.

I have the honour, Ma'am, to remain
your most obedient servant,

Constance

The Dowager Lady Crabtree

This diary belongs to:

Christian names __Elizabeth Alexandra Mary__
Surname __Mountbatten-Windsor__
Address __Buckingham Palace,__
__Windsor Castle, Sandringham House, Balmoral Castle__
Telephone no. __01-930 4832__

Father __Papa__
Mother __Mummy__
Next of kin __Philip__

Blood group __Blue__
Passport no. __Don't need one__
Occupation __Queen__

Height __5'4"__
Weight __9 stone 2 lbs after a state banquet__
Shoe size __5 (after a walkabout, 6)__

Bank account __Ask Keeper of the Privy Purse__

BIRTHDAYS

Mine: 21 April and 11 June   Mummy: 4 August
Philip: 10 June   Margaret: 21 August
Charles: 14 November   William: 21 June
Anne: 15 August   Harry: 15 September
Andrew: 19 February   Peter: 13 November
Edward: 10 March   Zara: 15 May
Diana: 1 July   David: 3 November
Sarah: 15 October   Sarah: 1 May
                    (A-J)

1953

I'm so worried. Such a short time to go . . . it's preying on my mind so much I can't think about anything else. I know that by the end of the week it will all be over, but if Aureole doesn't win the Derby on Saturday I shall be devastated. I'm a little bit anxious about the Coronation tomorrow too, which doesn't help.

I felt such a fool today, having to dash off to the bathroom in the middle of rehearsal in the Abbey. Simply everything seemed to be going wrong, and when I dropped the orb on the archbishop's foot I could have died. He let out a great yell and a ghastly string of rude words! Philip roared with laughter, but Mummy and I were quite shocked. Then when the Imperial State crown was placed on my head it slipped right down over my eyes. The Earl Marshal, the dear Duke of Norfolk, said he'd have some cotton wool put inside: I hope this does the trick – I shall look so silly if it wobbles, or gradually works its way down my forehead.

They've given me some special pills that will stop me wanting to spend a penny during the long ceremony, but I can't be sure they'll work. What worries me even more is having to remember who everybody is. It doesn't matter too much about the foreigners, because most of them can't understand me anyway, but what about all those maids of honour? How can I possibly be expected to recall names like Lady Jane Vane-Tempest-Stewart and Lady Jane Heathcote-Drummond-Willoughby? Mummy advises me just to smile and, when in doubt, wave. That's not so easy with an orb in one hand and a sceptre in the other. And what happens if my nose itches?

Oh, how right Shakespeare was when he wrote, 'Uneasy lies the head that wears the crown.'

Bobo's just brought the cocoa and I can hear Philip snoring already – it's all right for him. So I suppose I had better try to get some sleep. Thank goodness this only happens once in a reign.

CLARENCE HOUSE
S.W.1

My dearest Lilibet

31st May 1953

You have now been reigning for seventeen months, but in two days'
time you will be publicly crowned Queen - no backing out after that. Your
dear Papa and I were on the throne for seventeen years, and as your
Coronation draws near I feel it my duty to offer you a few tips on being Queen.
You know that I have never been one to interfere, but having observed your
conduct during these past months I feel that a few words of advice could prove
timely.

1. When Mr Churchill comes for his weekly audience, don't wear your slippers
    - it's a shade too informal, even if you _are_ in your own home.

2. When selecting your wardrobe, stick to what is plain and comfortable.
    People expect _me_ to look glamorous, and we don't want anybody saying
    that you dress just like your mother.

3. In the years to come, try to make sure that the Civil List keeps pace
    with the cost of living. The price of fur stoles and feathers has risen
    dramatically since clothes-rationing ended.

4. If you have a morning engagement, have only one cup of tea at breakfast
    and visit the bathroom immediately before leaving. It can save a lot of
    embarrassment later. Also, we don't want any nasty commercial opportun-
    ism. Someone once auctioned a lavatory seat I had sat on, and I'd hate
    that to happen ever again.

5. When you meet people for the first time always mention the weather.
    They expect it of you. If they are foreign tell them about the London
    fog. Never let on that it's nothing like as bad as it used to be. If lost
    for something to say, ask about _their_ weather.

6. When holding a state banquet, always include Margaret on the guest list,
    and try to pair her up with someone who is suitably eligible. Always
    be punctual, otherwise the guests will drink too much gin. Never talk

about the food. There is no point everyone airing their likes and dislikes when it is impossible to alter the menu.

7. Never talk about religion. Nobody expects it from the Head of the Church. Never talk about politics - leave that to the middle classes. Never talk about blood sports. Someone is bound to ask if Philip bagged a decent brace of pheasants on his last day's shooting. Never talk about money - they might ask for a loan.

8. Don't tell jokes. Philip's are quite enough for the two of you.

9. When meeting foreigners (someone not English) simply smile and nod while they are talking, looking down at the floor from time to time. Never laugh until they do. Introduce them to somebody else as soon as possible.

10. Always carry a good-sized handbag. It gives one something to do with one's hands, and it's always a good idea to have a half-bottle of brandy and a pack of cards handy for the car journey.

Finally, always think before you act. Remember that time in 1947 when I hit that Zulu chief over the head with an umbrella, thinking he was about to attack us when he was in fact offering us a ten-shilling note? Let that be a lesson to you: assume that everyone approaches in the spirit of friendship, and let the security people make sure they do.

I hope that you will find these tips helpful, my dear, as you embark upon this great voyage of your life.

I'll be praying for you on Tuesday.

Love and God bless,

Mummy xx

P.S. Did the doctor say that operation on Charles' ears could be done on the National Health?

2 June 1953   *Buckingham Palace*

For over a year I have imagined what it would be like and
now, suddenly, it's all over. I think Bobo must have slipped
something in my cocoa, because I slept quite well despite the
fact that 30,000 people were spending the night outside in The
Mall, singing and having a very jolly time. I felt a little sorry
for them because it poured with rain most of the night. In fact
it's rained for most of the day, too. 'Queen's weather,' they've
called it. Philip made some quip about me 'reigning constantly'
too, which we could have done without.

We got up at six this morning as the curlers had to be in my
hair for at least a couple of hours before I could get dressed.
Philip devoured a huge breakfast of bacon, kidneys, fried
bread, scrambled eggs and kippers. I confined myself to one
cup of tea, but after reading in the newspaper that one-quarter
of the world's population would be able to see and hear the
ceremony on film, television or radio I had a piece of toast too.
A rumbling tummy would have been too embarrassing for
words.

After the hairdresser had been, I was made up. They'd
invented a new lipstick called 'Balmoral Red', which is rather
ghastly but will make my mouth show up in black and white. I
spoke to Mummy on the telephone. She is a little concerned
because it seems so many sandwiches have been made for
street parties that the country now has a bread shortage. I
didn't tell Philip, because he'd only start quoting Marie-
Antoinette.

Received the news that a 34-year-old New Zealand bee
farmer called Edmund Hillary has become the first person to
reach the summit of Everest. I must knight him for the
achievement, of course, but I just hope that they don't expect
me to include Everest in the Commonwealth tour now. The
thought of climbing a mountain in sling-backs is a bit
worrying.

I put on my Coronation dress – very heavy, and very hot to
wear – at 10 o'clock. Unfortunately Norman Hartnell had left
a few pins in it, which gave me a few surprises throughout the
day. Then I said goodbye to Anne, who'd been shut in the

nursery, and the little mite kicked the rocking-horse as I tried to leave without her.

A few minutes later I climbed into the Coronation coach – not without misgivings, as it's pretty ancient and hasn't been used for sixteen years. I wish they'd told me about the special bracket they'd put in to hold the orb on the return journey – I sat with it sticking in my back all the way to the Abbey.

We arrived there a couple of minutes before eleven. I was joined by the maids of honour and the two bishops and we began the procession. The choir sang, 'I Was Glad', which made me very happy for them – but I didn't quite catch what they were so thrilled about.

When I arrived at the Coronation chair the archbishop presented me to the people and pointed me to all four corners of the Abbey – east, south, west and north. I felt I should have been blindfolded for this, then I could have shouted 'Coming – ready or not' afterwards. When I faced north I was confronted with a barrage of journalists yelling 'God save Queen Elizabeth' in a drunken haze. They'd been sitting in their seats for four hours already, no doubt sustained by the contents of their hip-flasks.

I then took the Oath on the Bible and swore to govern my realms according to their respective laws and customs. I couldn't help but remember the rehearsal for this, when the archbishop had appeared in slippers and torn surplice, clutching his pipe anxiously.

The choir sang Handel's 'Zadok the Priest', one of my favourite tunes, while the maids of honour took off my robes and jewellery. A canopy was held over my head for the next part, which I was dreading – the anointing. Philip had convinced me that they would use the goose-grease first used in 973 for the coronation of Edgar the Peaceful. I was pleasantly surprised when the archbishop used a rather fragrant oil, concocted by Mr Jamieson, my Bond Street chemist, from orange flowers, roses, cinnamon, jasmine, sesame, musk, civet and ambergris. I wouldn't mind laying in a stock of that for my bathroom.

Then came the most moving part of the ceremony, when I

was invested with the symbols of Queenship (Mummy always called them her 'props'). First the orb, a solid gold ball, representing the world, with a cross on top. This was no doubt designed by a man who thought that as long as it weighed pretty well as much as the whole world it would be a fair representation. I had to hold this dead weight in one hand and the sceptre, which was just as heavy, in the other.

Finally the royal ring – the 'wedding ring of England' – was placed on my finger. I was very careful to watch that this was put on correctly: Queen Victoria had it forced on to the wrong finger by a clumsy archbishop and it took three footmen and a bar of soap to remove it.

Then came the moment of crowning. The archbishop raised the glittering St Edward's crown high in the air, I bowed my head and very slowly it descended upon me (at precisely 12.33 and 30 seconds, according to Philip – he seemed to be studying his watch through the whole proceedings). My main concern was that it would stay in place without flattening my hair-do – Cecil Beaton was scheduled to do a photographic session with me in the afternoon. Suddenly all the peers put on their coronets and shouted, 'God save the Queen', trumpets blared, the Abbey bells rang, guns fired salutes all over London . . . and I felt tears spring to my eyes. One of Norman's pins was digging right into my back.

After the ceremony I changed into the Imperial State crown, which had been cleverly padded and fitted quite well, Though still heavy, being made of silver with inset diamonds, it was much lighter than the St Edward's crown, which is gold and weighs 5 lbs. It is a great shame that I will never be able to wear that one again. My son Charles will be the next to wear it, which seems strange at present when he's only four years old. I hope that it won't be for some time: at the moment the crown would completely envelop him, which wouldn't look at all regal. He was so good throughout the Coronation, sitting next to Mummy. I think she was secretly slipping him toffees to keep him quiet.

Philip and I then drove for an hour around the city in the Coronation coach so that the people could see me. I was very glad of that bracket for the orb at that stage – though to spectators it would have looked as if I was holding it.

By the time we got back to Buckingham Palace I was desperate for a cup of tea and a chance to visit the powder room. Then began a succession of appearances on the balcony and a Royal Air Force fly-past. Fortunately the sun had come out by this time, but by then thousands were soaked to the skin after waiting there all day. Mummy said that the weather had been even worse when she was crowned.

I was quite astounded by the throngs of people outside Buckingham Palace – a mass of heaving humanity as far as the eye could see. The Lord Chamberlain estimated that there were half a million or so. I remember Daddy saying after Grandfather's Silver Jubilee that he hadn't realized how much he was loved until he saw the crowds. I know exactly how he felt.

I brought Anne out on to the balcony, which seemed a popular decision, but she could hardly see over the edge and slipped out of sight rather frequently. As all the family dashed into the Chinese Luncheon Room for tea and sandwiches, I had a long photographic session with Cecil then made a number of solo appearances on the balcony, and finally a speech to the nation. Later I collapsed in front of the television to watch a special edition of Television Newsreel, then joined the family for fireworks in the garden at half past ten.

It is now 2 o'clock in the morning and Bobo is insisting that I go to sleep. I'm on my fifth cup of cocoa, but I'm just too elated to relax. What an incredibly wonderful day it's been! I just hope I can live up to everyone's expectations of me.

6 June 1953   *Windsor Castle*
Aureole *lost* the Derby! All those months of training wasted. I was very upset – after all, I'd chosen his name specially because I thought that he would win me a lot of gold. Everyone congratulated me on the fact that he came in second, but it would have been better for him not to have been placed at all than to come so close.

It was rather irritating to have to present the cup to the

winning jockey, Sir Gordon Richards. I *knew* I should never have knighted him in the Coronation Honours. Still, it was his 29th attempt, so I suppose he deserved something for determination. Richards and his trainer, Norman Bertie, came to see me in the royal box.

'Congratulations, Mr Bertie, on winning the Derby,' I said.

'May I congratulate you, Your Majesty, on winning the world,' he replied. What an odd thing to have said. I was a little taken aback. There wasn't a lot I could say, so I smiled broadly and ushered them towards the champagne.

Philip hasn't helped matters by being in a bad mood all day. I think it's because so many Coronation guests are rather outstaying their welcome. Over a hundred of us sat down to breakfast this morning; it was more like a state banquet. I dread to think how much marmalade we got through.

'We never seem to have the Castle to ourselves,' he moaned.

9 June 1953   *Buckingham Palace*
Mummy and Margaret both have bad colds, which they blame on the draughts of Westminster Abbey last week. They're both due to visit Southern Rhodesia soon, so I hope they'll have recovered by then. Margaret seems determined not to go. I wish I knew why – I'm sure there's some reason that she hasn't told us about.

Mr Churchill came for his weekly audience and broke down in tears. He still gets very emotional whenever the Coronation is mentioned. He's a very dear man, but I can't help wondering if 79 isn't a bit old to be Prime Minister. He keeps quoting Gladstone and Disraeli at me.

11 June 1953   *Buckingham Palace*
Trooped the Colour. Bobo has started packing for our Commonwealth tour . . . Had tea with Mummy and Margaret at Clarence House – the first time that I have really had a chance to look at our old home since they moved in last May. There have certainly been a few changes since Philip and I lived there, and not always for the better in my opinion. There's now a small bar in the drawing-room, which seems

quite out of character with the otherwise chintzy ambience. I didn't like to mention it, but it does look rather common.

Margaret was in a particularly roguish mood, and has taken to smoking Woodbines. It wouldn't have been quite so bad if, once she'd run out, she hadn't reached for a packet of Rizla and started rolling her own – a nasty habit that she picked up from Gan-Gan.[1] I was a little concerned to hear that she and Mummy had gone *incognita* to the theatre last night – that thriller at the Ambassadors called *The Mousetrap*; Margaret says that as it's been running for seven months they wanted to see it before it closed, but why couldn't they have gone officially? They're like a couple of schoolgirls sometimes. I couldn't help noticing how Mummy pushed the newspapers under the sofa as I arrived. I know that she likes to sit and chat, but I've not seen a paper for days.

14 June 1953   *Windsor Castle*
House-party gathered here for Ascot, but the day was marred for me when Tommy[2] brought me a copy of *The People* this morning. It says that Margaret is in love with Group Captain Peter Townsend, the new Comptroller of the Household at Clarence House. I've been hearing rumours for weeks but thought it was just gossip amongst the Pages of the Backstairs. Those boys can be bitchy at the best of times. They say it's been going on since 1948! How can I not have noticed?

'The story is of course utterly untrue. It is quite unthinkable that a royal princess, third in line of succession to the throne, should even contemplate marriage with a man who has been through the divorce courts,' says the article. I ran along to Margaret's room and confronted her with it.

'Yes, Lilibet, it's true,' she said, very matter-of-factly, puffing cigarette smoke in my face. 'I want to marry him.'

I moved her gold lamé dressing-gown from the bed and sat down heavily.

[1]Queen Mary.
[2]Rt. Hon. Sir Alan Lascelles, the Queen's Private Secretary.

'But he's divorced, Margo,' I said. 'You know what divorce means in our family . . .'

'Abdication,' she sneered.

I tried to explain the Royal Marriages Act of 1772, but Margaret is never at her best before midday on a Sunday.

The news of this romance has been worrying me all day. I didn't even feel like playing charades this evening.

'Let her get on with it,' Philip remarked. 'You know, Chips Channon says she has a Marie-Antoinette aroma about her.'

What Margaret's perfume has to do with it I have no idea . . .

15 June 1953   *Windsor Castle*

Spoke to Richard Colville, my Press Secretary, who agrees that we must avoid a scandal at all costs. Sent Tommy round to Downing Street to discuss the situation with the PM. It must be hushed up as soon as possible so that we can enjoy Ascot week in peace. I don't think Mr Churchill understood the situation at all.

'What a delightful match! A lovely young royal lady married to a gallant young airman, safe from the perils and horrors of war . . .' He's such an old fool.

When the predicament was explained to him, he began to moralize. Apparently Mrs Churchill was listening in on the conversation and couldn't remain silent when she heard him.

'Winston!' she exclaimed, 'if you are going to begin the Abdication all over again, I'm going to leave. I shall take a flat and go and live in Brighton.'

I don't know if she's serious, but we can't possibly have another scandal on top of the Margaret/Peter one.

I tried reasoning with Margaret – everything from telling her that Peter is far too old for her to explaining that she will look like a midget beside him. Only when I suggested that he was virtually teetotal and would certainly make her give up cigarettes did she show any signs of doubt.

Whilst Bobo was helping me undress tonight she suggested that we begin our Commonwealth tour early to get away from all this. Dear Bobo, she always has an answer for everything.

17 June 1953   *Windsor Castle*

It's all agreed! Peter Townsend has promised to accept the post of Air Attaché in Brussels at once, and he and Margaret have agreed not to see each other for at least one year. If she still loves him then I'll have to see if I can discreetly amend the Royal Marriages Act in the next Parliament. Perhaps it can be done under another name and slipped in unnoticed. Either way we have twelve months' breathing space, and at least I can enjoy Ascot in peace. I've entered Aureole for the King George VI and Queen Elizabeth stakes, hoping we can nobble Gordon Richards this time.

BUCKINGHAM PALACE

23-VII-53

<u>Milkman</u>
2,597 PINTS TODAY, PLEASE
and ½ DOZEN EGGS.
Thank you.

BUCKINGHAM PALACE

MEMORANDUM TO YEOMAN OF THE SILVER PANTRY

Please use stainless steel teaspoons for today's Garden Party. Last week 2,008 of my best crested spoons disappeared in the pockets and handbags of souvenir hunters. This has got to stop. Arrange to borrow some from Victoria Station – BR are used to losing them.

Didn't they come last year!
EIIR

EⅡR

The Lord Chamberlain is
commanded by Her Majesty to invite

....

...........*Mr. and Mrs. John Smith*...........

to a Garden Party at Buckingham Palace
on Thursday, 23 July 1953, at 2.00 p.m.
R.S.V.P.

23 July 1953   *Buckingham Palace*

The last garden party of the season, thank goodness. We left the Bow Room at four o'clock and made our way as quickly as possible to the tea tent. So *many* people to speak to, though, and I got very irritated by being told, by all of them, how nice I'd looked on the 'telly' during the Coronation. Other than that the only subject seemed to be the fact that Aureole lost at Ascot, of which I didn't care to be reminded.

Managed to get back in time for Charles' and Anne's baths. We're putting them both in together at the moment as this saves time, although there's a limit as to how long we can go on doing this as Anne is very inquisitive. Charles is becoming rather subdued these days, ever since we told him that he is to begin having school lessons this autumn. Miss Peebles is to teach him in the nursery, so he should be all right. 'Mispy', as he calls her, or is it 'Miss P.'?, is very strict and should be an excellent tutor for him. I've told her that she must stop him using his bed as a trampoline, and to teach him economics. If only he knew how much garden parties cost nowadays, he wouldn't take everything for granted.

5 August 1953   *Balmoral Castle*

At last Philip and I have managed to escape to Balmoral. So nice to have the place to ourselves – just Charles, Anne, me and 62 staff. Bobo is *still* packing for our Commonwealth tour.

Had a visit from Norman Hartnell this morning before we left, bringing me a few more dress designs for the tour. I had previously told him to be a little more adventurous, which was probably a mistake as some of the ideas he submitted were verging on the outrageous. I had thought it would be nice to wear the colours of each country that I visit, or have its emblem incorporated in the dress material, but Norman seemed to have taken this idea literally. I didn't really mind the boomerang-and-kiwi-fruit design on the suit for Australia, but I did draw the line at the Carmen Miranda outfit, complete with the fruit-bowl hat, for Ceylon. As for the grass skirt and coconut bodice he had visualized for my trip to Tonga, well, words failed me for a moment, but I'm sure he gathered from my silence that this really wasn't on. I also refused to have a Union Flag motif on the dress for our return to London. I may be Queen of England, but I refuse to sail down the Thames on the royal barge looking like Britannia.

I told him that we would stick with the 'New Look', which has suited me for years.

Had a postcard from Princess Marina – she would like to come and stay for six weeks; and a note from Princess Margaret asking whether there is a cocktail shaker here or whether she should bring one. I don't think we have one on the staff, but could possibly get a ghillie from the estate to come in and do it.

19 November 1953   *Buckingham Palace*

The Prime Minister persuaded me to give Royal Assent to the Regency Act, which will mean that if anything happens to me Philip can act as Prince Regent until Charles is old enough to be king. This is all very well in theory, but I was a bit disturbed to find Philip trying on one of my tiaras as I came out of my dressing-room this morning. I think his valet, John, had encouraged him to do it, but his quips about bumping me off are no longer amusing. I gave him one of my frosty looks and had Bobo bring supper to me on a tray, with the excuse that I had to get my Christmas cards written before we go away.

Finally got some of the Coronation photos back from the chemist, so I can pass the time on the long voyages ahead sticking those in my album. One month from today we shall be with Queen Salote in Tonga. I do hope that she won't have one of her ritual banquets. I lose my appetite having to stare at an overflowing mound (of food, I mean, not Queen Salote), and I find a whole sucking-pig on my plate just too much.

I hear that she was so enchanted by our black London taxi cabs when she came to England for the Coronation that she has ordered one for herself. I hope she won't expect *me* to travel in it.

23 November 1953   *Strato-cruiser* Canopus

Left London Airport today to begin our six-month tour of the Commonwealth. Bobo was still packing right up to the time of our departure, so I do hope that she hasn't forgotten anything. All my luggage has yellow labels and Philip's are mauve; that way if the natives cannot read our names they can at least tell the difference between our cases. Knowing our luck, we'll probably have colour-blind porters.

Mummy, Margaret and Mr Churchill came to see us off, which was very sad. I was near to tears when I had to leave Charles and little Anne behind, but then I remembered Queen Mary's words, 'Duty, Lilibet!' and I bit my lip as she had taught me.

Today's *Daily Mirror* had a strange article saying that Charles should be allowed to mix with working-class people and that Buckingham Palace should be open to the public. What do they want me to do? Send Charles down the mines and open the Palace as an hotel?

Played 'I-Spy' with two ladies-in-waiting, but there's not much to see at 18,000 feet. They kept choosing 'clouds' and 'sky'; I kept pretending that I didn't know the answer just to keep them happy. Is this what being Queen is all about?

25 December 1953   *Government House, Auckland*

What a strange Christmas! Mince pies, Christmas pudding and Father Christmas all in the brilliant New Zealand sun. When Philip sang 'I'm Dreaming of a White Christmas' in the bath this morning I felt quite homesick. I can't hear him singing in the bath at the Palace.

Telephoned Mummy and Margaret. Margaret was at a party, and Mummy herself sounded very merry. I then spoke to Charles and Anne. They were very excited – Charles asked me who I was, and then Anne said a *very* rude word. I don't know where she picked that up, but it will have to stop. No 3-year-old should know about such activities.

Made my Christmas broadcast, declaring that I wanted to show that the Crown is not merely an abstract symbol of our unity but a personal and living bond between us all: Michael Adeane's words, but they sounded good. I said how completely and most happily at home I felt, and saw Philip mouthing the word 'liar!'

Saw lots of Maori dancing and had to wear a very itchy cloak of kiwi feathers. The Maoris call me the 'Rare White Heron of the Single Flight' – Heaven only knows why. Have made up my mind that I am going to spend next Christmas at Sandringham. Received some lovely presents from the family:

pearl necklace from Philip

pearl tiara from Mummy

pearl necklace (two rows) from Margaret

imitation pearl necklace from the Kents

one pearl earring (second to follow on my birthday) from the Gloucesters

pearl, diamond, emerald and ruby brooch, necklace and earrings from Uncle David & Auntie Wallis

thread-it-yourself pearl necklace kit from Aunt Mary (Princess Royal)

mother-of-pearl grape scissors from Bobo (dear Bobo, she always buys me something practical)

1954

25 February 1954   *Melbourne, Victoria*

The 95th day of our Commonwealth tour and I'm beginning to feel just a little weary. Opened my fourth parliament this month and wore my Coronation dress yet again. People will begin to think that I've got nothing else to wear. I enjoy wearing it but it gets so hot. The sun is so strong here that I have to move the position of the pearls discreetly when nobody is looking to avoid getting a white mark round my neck and keep the suntan even. The crowds are very boisterous here and shout 'Good on yer, Liz!' from the tops of trees and roofs.

I'm getting very expert now at dodging Union flags as children wave them at me and try to stick them up my nose, but I do find it a great strain to smile all the time. Today I travelled in a motorcade for 1 hour 45 minutes. For many it is the only time in their life that they will see their Queen and they expect me to look happy, but if I try to maintain the smile I get a twitch, so I stop for a second. The moment I stop, a journalist or photographer catches me and the next day the papers say I look cross.

We'd only been here a few minutes before Philip caused an upset. We were sitting beside a microphone, which had accidentally been left on during an ethnic fertility dance, when he turned to me and said, 'Don't look so sad, Sausage,' which was meant for my ears only. *Everybody* heard. The papers will be full of that tomorrow, I suppose.

Received a postcard from Margaret. They've had gales in Britain with 90-mile-an-hour winds, so there are some blessings in being here.

While I was doing the boxes this afternoon I saw that they are proposing to put the TV licence up to £3 a year on 1 June. Perhaps we should stick with the wireless – the programmes are better. I'm missing *Mrs Dale's Diary* out here. I think Jim's been overdoing it, but I shan't find out whether he's all right until we get back.

20 March 1954   *On board the SS* Gothic
Outbreak of polio in Australia. Philip and I were inoculated in
Canberra, but it seemed like a good excuse not to shake any
more hands. Already it has been calculated that I have
listened to 276 speeches, heard 'God Save the Queen' sung 508
times, made 102 speeches myself, been curtsied to 6,770 times
and shaken (so far) 13,213 hands. I'm going to write to *The
Guinness Book of Records* just as soon as we get home. We've
also received 197 gifts, most of them very strange, including a
cattle whip twice as long as Philip, a model of the Rock of
Gibraltar, and a lavatory brush in the shape of a wallaby. In
return we've given the usual framed photographs of ourselves.
Bobo signs them for me as my arm aches after a day of
constant waving.

1 May 1954   *Tobruk*
Spending the day with King Idris of Libya. He knew of my
love of dogs and promised a surprise. I'm not certain what the
meat was at lunch, but it tasted decidedly unusual.
   Stood on his balcony, which was not as big as ours, to watch
the Royal Yacht *Britannia* bringing Charles and Anne from
England. They have both grown so much! Charles is turning
into a very mature boy and can read all by himself now. I do
hope we can find an ear specialist when we get home.

POST   CARD

7-5-54
Dear Lilibet.
Have just been down a coal mine.
Tomorrow I'm opening a sewerage farm
then touring an artificial limb plant.
Can we have a word about my bloody
awful engagement diary as soon as
you get home?! Mummy says
she hopes you're wearing a vest.
Love, Margo.

Calverton Colliery, Nottingham

10 May 1954   *Gibraltar*

Had a civic luncheon and reviewed the troops. Went with the children to see the apes. Philip embarrassed me by looking at the gathered press photographers and asking in a loud voice which were the apes as he threw peanuts at them.

15 May 1954   *Buckingham Palace*

Returned to London after 173 days away. How wonderful to be in England, and *what* a welcome from the people! It was extremely touching. From the Channel to the Thames we were greeted by ships of the Home Fleet and hundreds of smaller vessels.

Sir Winston Churchill joined us at the Isle of Wight and was very emotional at seeing me again, although he had a very bad cold so kept his distance. Philip gave him the exploding cigars that we had bought in Malta as a joke, which was probably a mistake. In return Winston gave us the V for Victory sign, so he obviously shares my husband's sense of humour.

Winston described the Thames as we sailed down it as 'the silver thread that runs through the history of Britain'. It looked like a dirty commercial river to me, but how touching that he sees things so romantically.

Mummy and Margaret came on board to welcome us. Margaret told me that I had put on weight. So would she have done if she'd had to eat as many sucking-pigs and drink as much coconut milk and wombat secretions as I have!

Travelled in state landau back to Buckingham Palace through vast crowds. It was like the Coronation all over again. Made four appearances on the balcony with Charles and Anne tonight. Retired to bed early to catch up on the racing results. They still haven't replaced that light bulb over my bed. Bobo busy unpacking.

10 June 1954   *Buckingham Palace*

Trooped the Colour. Bobo still unpacking . . .

18 June 1954   *Windsor Castle*

The last day of Ascot and I had two wins! At *last* Aureole won the King George VI and Queen Elizabeth stakes. Received Herr Julius Raab, the Austrian Chancellor; how fortunate that we were able to discuss horses today rather than the war. Food rationing has officially ended, so we had a state banquet without feeling guilty.

Heard a wonderful story over dinner about the PM. Sir Winston was entertaining the Prime Minister of Pakistan and asked him if he would like a whisky and soda.

'No, thank you,' replied the Pakistani Prime Minister.

'What's that?' asked Winston.

'No, thank you.'

'What, why?'

'I'm a teetotaller, Mr Churchill.'

'What's that?'

'I'm a teetotaller.'

'A teetotaller. Christ! I mean God! I mean Allah!'

At this point an astonished footman dropped his tray of drinks, but caught it before it reached the carpet! We ought to put him in the England cricket team.

14 October 1954   *Windsor Castle*

Installed Anthony Eden as a Knight of the Garter. Thought I'd better, in view of the fact that he could well be the next Prime Minister. I do hope so as he is rather attractive, and I would appreciate a younger leader of my Government. Winston is a very nice man, but I still feel a little intimidated by him and the smell of his cigar lingers for days after his weekly audience. I mentioned the Anglo-Egyptian Suez Canal Agreement to him today and he began reminiscing about a barge holiday he and Lady Churchill had on a canal in 1927. I now spend most audiences discussing horses with him, which seems to keep him amused. Saw Margaret eyeing up the Master of the Household today – she's always so friendly with the staff.

25 December 1954   *Sandringham House*

So nice to spend Christmas at dear old Sandringham, even if it is damp and draughty. Couldn't eat any lunch as I was so worried about doing my broadcast at 3 o'clock. It's all right for everybody else – they can all tuck in and have a very jolly feast, but *I* had to lock myself in a bathroom to rehearse. In the end the speech went very well, despite Philip's attempts to make me laugh by lying on the floor and tickling my feet. I could feel my voice going higher and higher as I tried to ignore him. They mentioned that I could in future do my speech on television, but really it's bad enough doing it on radio.

   Arguments this evening over which games to play. Margaret wanted to play postman's knock, Mummy was all for gin rummy and Philip wanted to play strip poker, whatever that is. Instead I overruled them and we watched the Duke of Gloucester's lovely home movie of the Coronation, which everyone seemed to enjoy because they all cheered very loudly when we reached the last reel of film.

1955

1 January 1955   *Sandringham House*

New Year's Resolutions:

1. Will stop laying foundation stones. My back aches for days afterwards.
2. Cut down on planting trees. White gloves get so dirty.
3. Will stop wearing magenta. It doesn't suit me.
4. Must resist putting more than 5 shillings on every horse I back.
5. Will try to stop making speeches after family lunches.

Lost my address book today; now I haven't the slightest idea who my friends are.

4 January 1955   *Sandringham House*

Philip has returned to London for a couple of days as he had some engagements to carry out, but he sent me a note to let me know he's thinking about me. At least I *think* it's me he had in mind . . .

BUCKINGHAM PALACE

4th January 1955

Dearest Lilibet,

I know that you were rather hurt recently by comments in the press that your speeches are dull, but people do like to be entertained. In a few months' time we'll have Independent Television to compete with as well, so we must think up a few new catchphrases for ourselves.

Meanwhile, here are a few one-liners for you to drop into your speeches, to liven them up. Maybe we should get Arthur Askey or Bud Flanagan to come and give you a few hints on timing, too.

I'm sure the public is ready for a monarch with a sense of humour.

All my love, Philip

All-purpose opening line: 'A funny thing happened to me on the way from the Palace.'

For the Fruit Growers' Association: 'My sister eats lots of fruit. She has at least three cherries in every martini.'

For any gathering of the medical profession: 'Medical scientists claim that whisky cannot cure the common cold... but then neither can medical science.'
                                        (Controversial, what?)

For the Jockey Club: 'I've named one of my horses "Radish". Now I can say, "Here's my horse Radish."'

For the Annual Playwrights' Awards Ceremony: 'All work and no play is the occupational hazard of a dramatist.'

For television moguls: 'Television enables people with nothing to do to watch people who can do nothing.'

And here are some opening lines for when you meet people for the first time:

'What do you do for a living? You are living, aren't you?'

'What a lovely fur coat! Did you kill it yourself?'

'I never forget a face — but in your case I'll make an exception.'

'Have you been waiting long, or do you always stand like that?'

4 April 1955   *Buckingham Palace*
Farewell dinner at 10 Downing Street given by the Churchills
to mark Winston's resignation. Decided to give him the full
treatment with the outfit and got Bobo to polish up Queen
Mary's elegant bow-knot tiara, which I don't often wear as it
digs into my head at the back, but it looks good. Must get
Garrard's to adjust it. Wore a sash and as many decorations as
could tastefully adorn it. Philip didn't want to go. When I
asked him how we should dress, he said, 'Very, very slowly,
then we might not get there at all.' He can be so wicked at
times.

Winston and Clemmie were on the steps of Number 10 to
greet us.

'I've just had my carbuncles treated with X-rays, Ma'am,'
said Winston as we walked up the staircase.

'How very nice for you,' I smiled.

'Virulent microbes, but not malignant,' he added.

I suddenly lost my appetite. Thank heavens the newspaper
strike is still on and none of our conversations can be
reported. Over dinner he asked me to delay appointing Sir
Anthony Eden Prime Minister, just to keep him on his toes.
Why must I always play cat and mouse?

Spilt potato on my sash. Fortunately it was amongst the
decorations, so it may have looked like part of my brooch.

31 May 1955   *Buckingham Palace*
Had to declare a state of emergency because of the rail strike.
Eden may officially be PM now, but the country seems no
better for it. It's a jolly good excuse to cancel Trooping the
Colour this year, although I fear that Ascot may have to go as
well. Damn.

16 June 1955   *Royal Lodge, Windsor*
Spent a relaxing day looking round the mausoleum at
Frogmore amongst my ancestors. Then had tea with Mummy,
who always serves a delicious tipsy cake. In one of her women's
magazines we noticed the most amusing article by my ex-

governess Marion Crawford. Mummy has never forgiven her for writing a book about us and always refers to her in the most unladylike terms. In the magazine Crawfie had written all about this year's Trooping the Colour and Ascot, neither of which happened, giving a blow-by-blow account of all that took place. Mummy choked on a piece of battenberg when she read the colourful description of the non-existent events. Three footmen, a Page of the Presence and the Duke of Kent thumped her on the back, but neither that nor three cups of Earl Grey seemed to dislodge it. Fortunately Mummy had a small hip-flask of special medicine in her handbag, which seemed to do the trick.

'How dare old Crabfeatures write about us again!' she gasped as they carried her into the house.

20 August 1955   *Castle of Mey*

The floodlights that Mummy had erected in honour of Anne's fifth birthday have been retained for Margaret's twenty-fifth birthday tomorrow. She still insists that she wants to marry Peter Townsend (Margaret, not Mummy) and everyone is gossiping about it. 'Come on, Margaret! Make your mind up!' said the *Daily Mirror* yesterday, as if it were any business of theirs. Had just decided that I should let them spend as much time together as possible, which is the simplest way of putting an end to any relationship, when I had a telephone call from the Archbishop of Canterbury.

'What can I do for you, Geoffrey?' I asked. 'If it's to wish Princess Margaret happy birthday, that's not until tomorrow.'

'From an ecclesiastical point of view, Your Majesty, I must urge you to remember that if your sister were to marry Peter Townsend and anything were to happen to Prince Charles and Princess Anne, her children by the union would make the royal line illegitimate.'

Why is everyone in this world obsessed with Margaret and Peter?

'Thank you, Geoffrey, that's been a great help,' I said. I hope I didn't sound too insincere.

30 October 1955   *Buckingham Palace*

I've decided that enough is enough. Philip said in bed last night, 'You're Queen, put your foot down. If you can't, who can?' Perhaps he's right. But who is a queen to turn to for advice? After sleeping on it, I decided there and then to put an end to it all. First I had an audience with Sir Anthony Eden, but he's in no position to comment either way. Just like Townsend, he was the innocent party in a divorce and is now married to Clarissa Churchill. How could he possibly condemn the immorality of it all? I sent for the car and was driven to Clarence House.

'No, I've not come to watch the racing on television, Mummy,' I said. 'I've come to see Margaret.'

'About the "trouble"?' she mouthed, without actually saying the words, probably knowing that whatever she said would be through the staff restroom quicker than you can say 'Longchamps'.

'To put an *end* to the trouble,' I said firmly. 'Where is she?'

'Trying out my new billiard table.'

'Right,' I said. Then I told my lady-in-waiting to stay and chat to Mummy while I headed for the games room.

'Lilibet, darling,' said Margaret, breezily, blowing chalk dust in my face from the end of her billiard cue as if it were a six-shooter: 'Come to goad me about Peter, have you?' She looked at me menacingly.

'I haven't come to goad you . . .' I began.

'I expect you've got the Prime Minister, the entire Cabinet, half the House of Lords and a hangman outside in the hall waiting to lynch me. Well, I'm going to marry him, and that's final!'

'OK, Margo,' I said calmly, thinking carefully of the words that Philip had told me to say. 'Go ahead. Marry Peter.'

A billiard ball landed heavily on the floor, narrowly missing Whisky, one of Mummy's corgis.

'What did you say?'

'I said, go on, marry Peter.'

'And?'

'It's quite simple,' I said, putting on my Queen Victoria face.

'You will just have to give up public life totally, renounce your rights of succession and relinquish your Civil List income.'

'And become plain Margaret Townsend and live off his money?'

'Yes.'

She went rather pale and fell silent for a few minutes. Then she lit a cigarette and said, quite lightly, 'Well, Lilibet, never let it be said that the Queen's sister doesn't know where her duty lies.'

Margaret is to announce publicly tomorrow that she has decided not to marry Group Captain Peter Townsend.

1 November 1955   *Buckingham Palace*
Philip and I spent a relaxing evening watching television, while I did the boxes and wrote a speech. Saw an advertisement on the new Independent Television, showing a tube of Gibbs SR toothpaste in a block of ice. These so-called 'commercials' will never catch on. Bobo busy packing for my three-week tour of Nigeria. She complained that Anne and Charles were playing their gramophone record of 'Rock Around the Clock' too loudly. I told her that it was only Mr Haley and his Rockets and she must learn to move with the times. Poor old Bobo, she does so hate change.

1956

27 January 1956   *Lagos, Nigeria*

Just before our arrival today instructions were issued that hats have to be removed in front of the Queen. Thousands of my loyal but hatless subjects then rushed out and bought hats just so that they could whisk them off when they saw me. How endearing!

The air-conditioning here in my bedroom has gone wrong and it's like an icebox. In fact it's just like being back at Sandringham. Philip said we could do with having Harold Macmillan around to provide us with some hot air.

2 May 1956   *Windsor Castle*

Philip and I have decided to phase out the debutante balls. At first he enjoyed having row upon row of nubile young girls curtseying to him every year, but now, like me, he is beginning to find it all a bit tedious. They're all from the same class, which makes it terribly boring, and they seem to use me as some kind of status symbol. After long discussions with my aides it has been decided to ease off the court presentations over the next two years (to cut them out suddenly would disappoint so many on the waiting list) and bring in something we are going to call 'informal luncheons' for a broader-based group of people. Using the word 'informal' will make the occasions less intimidating for my guests, and we need only give them a cheap snack, some Harrod's sausages and a little fresh fruit, perhaps.

These lunches will enable me to meet people from all walks of life, really common people like actors and also members of the working class. Everyone will be vetted first, of course, just to make sure that they don't put their feet on the table or eat peas with their knife. Margaret sat next to somebody once who actually drank from his fingerbowl; it seems incredible that anyone could make such a mistake with an everyday household item.

28 July 1956   *Arundel Castle*

A very bad day at the races. We were all sitting in the Duke of Richmond's private box at Goodwood when suddenly a missive came from the PM asking that I sign a proclamation immediately to call out the Army just in case the Suez crisis gets worse. Missed the last race.

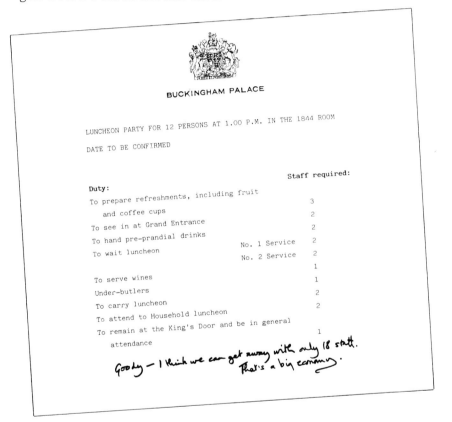

BUCKINGHAM PALACE

LUNCHEON PARTY FOR 12 PERSONS AT 1.00 P.M. IN THE 1844 ROOM

DATE TO BE CONFIRMED

Staff required:

Duty:

To prepare refreshments, including fruit	3
and coffee cups	2
To see in at Grand Entrance	2
To hand pre-prandial drinks	2
To wait luncheon No. 1 Service	2
No. 2 Service	1
To serve wines	1
Under-butlers	2
To carry luncheon	2
To attend to Household luncheon	
To remain at the King's Door and be in general attendance	1

Goody — I think we can get away with only 18 staff. That's a big economy.

1 August 1956   *Palace of Holyroodhouse*

Criticism in the press today that Philip does not seem to be actively pursuing his naval career, so we decided at the garden party this afternoon that he would put in four months just to keep them quiet. This evening while we were watching one of Armand and Michaela Denis's lovely wildlife programmes on television Philip decided that he would like to go to Malaya, New Zealand, Ceylon and the Gambia, then he can look at animals at the same time. I cannot believe that he really wants to go, but he's putting a very, very brave face on it.

17 October 1956   *Buckingham Palace*
Travelled up to Cumberland to open the world's first large-scale nuclear power station. Wore a dress in Electricity Board colours, but doubt anyone appreciated this.

20 November 1956   *Luton Hoo*
How sad that Philip and I have to be apart on our wedding anniversary. Spent the day with Aunt Zia and Uncle Harold.[1] Philip sent me a dozen white roses and a photograph he had taken of two iguanas with their arms around each other. What a sweet, romantic old thing he is.

31 December 1956   *Sandringham House*
Quite a jolly end to the year. I was feeling a bit sad at being apart from Philip, then Mummy suggested that we recount our racing successes of the year, which really cheered me up because it's been such a good one. I gathered all the family together in the White Drawing Room after dinner and told them again about Mulberry Harbour winning the Chelsea and the Newmarket Oaks (she was proclaimed the third-best-trained filly in England). Then, of course, Carrozza – niece of Sun Chariot – won the Epsom Oaks by only 9 inches, which was terribly exciting. Then to cap it all Almeria won the Ribblesdale Stakes at Ascot. She's a big animal and suffers from hypertension, but I have high hopes for her next year. I had scarcely begun to explain my breeding programme for 1957 when midnight chimed. The previous three hours had just flown by. Sadly, many of the family had been feeling so exhausted that they had had to retire to bed early, but at least Margo, Mummy and I saw the New Year in – even if Mummy was asleep.

[1] Sir Harold and Lady Anastasia Wernher.

Dearest Lilibet,

Here is the recipe for lemon barley water that you wanted. It goes quite well with gin, but I expect you will drink it on its own. It's particularly good if you've been conferring knighthoods or doing anything else that requires a lot of standing about.

ROYAL BARLEY WATER

¼ teacup pearl barley

4 pints boiling water

2 lemons

6 oranges

demerara sugar to taste

Get the kitchen staff to put the barley in a large saucepan, add the boiling water and simmer over a low heat into a basin, adding the rind of one lemon and three oranges. Add the sugar. Allow to stand until cold. Strain off the rinds and add the orange and lemon juice. When very cold, get an under-butler to pour it.

Love,
Mummy

1957

7 January 1957   *Sandringham House*

Sir Anthony Eden resigned due to ill health. I travelled to London to see him so that he needn't do the journey to Norfolk. To spare his feelings I thought I might fit in Harrods sale while I was at it. Dear 'Rab' Butler is going to stand in for the moment, which will be *such* fun. He has such a lived-in face and really knows what he's talking about. Churchill wanted me to appoint Macmillan.

'Is it to be Wab or Hawold?' asked Lord Salisbury at the Privy Council Meeting.

'Mr Butler,' I said.

Got back to Sandringham to find that Anne had tied Charles to the Christmas tree and locked Nanny in the attic. For a 7-year-old that girl is absolutely wild.

Told the Master of the Household to give the servants a rocket for not taking the tree down yesterday on Twelfth Night. Now we'll have bad luck all the year.

28 February 1957   *Sandringham House*

So nice to have Philip home. Was very excited and got a bit carried away by promising to make him a Prince of the United Kingdom. I don't suppose it will do any harm. Margaret sang 'Some Day My Prince Will Come' outside the bedroom door tonight, and I could have sworn I saw him blush.

7 April 1957   *Buckingham Palace*

Harold Macmillan is to be Prime Minister. He came to see me after lunch today, looking immaculate in his frock-coat.

'*Bonjour*, Monsieur Macmillan,' I said (I have been practising my French today in preparation for my state visit to France tomorrow).

We had a good audience. It seems that he loves shooting and enjoys country house parties, which is useful in a prime minister. We share the same doctor (Sir John Richardson), too, I discovered. I also noticed that he is extremely thrifty, asking if he could make a quick telephone call and thus save the Government 'a penny ha'penny' on the Downing Street bill. Before he left he told me that I should smile more. I thought people expected me to look serious. We decided to end National Service in 1960, which will mean Charles won't have to join up if he doesn't want to.

6 June 1957   *Buckingham Palace*
Finally had to concede and agree to my Christmas broadcast being televised. It's such a worry. We've had a woman called Sylvia Peters here today trying to show me the art of appearing on television. Also they have a new-fangled machine called a teleprompter for me to read from. I kept saying, 'I'm a queen, not a theatrical pro.' 'Some of us are both, ducky,' remarked one of the floor managers. What *can* he have meant?

Had to undress myself this evening as Bobo is packing for my visit to Canada and the United States of America.

19 October 1957   *New York*
My state visit to Canada and the United States has been ruined by Malcolm Muggeridge, whose article headlined 'DOES ENGLAND REALLY NEED A QUEEN?' was published today in the *Saturday Evening Post*.

Well, does a queen really need Malcolm Muggeridge, I ask myself when I read scurrilous articles like that. He used to be such a witty man when he was editor of *Punch*. I'd even got him on my list of possible knighthoods, but he's certainly blown that now. How dare he call us a royal soap opera, detached from the real world?

Bought a beautiful racehorse today, excellent for stud. Managed to knock the owner down to $35,000, which means I still have enough of my holiday money left to buy a few presents. Received a gift myself today – a gold-plated model of the Empire State Building. It will look lovely in the bathroom of guest suite 298 at Buckingham Palace.

21 October 1957   *Washington DC*

Met the British Ambassador to the USA at a reception. While we were there a journalist telephoned and asked him what wishes he had for Christmas. The Ambassador seemed very embarrassed and at first insisted that he wanted nothing. In the end he said, 'Well, if you insist, perhaps just a small box of crystallized fruit, thank you.'

What a sweet man.

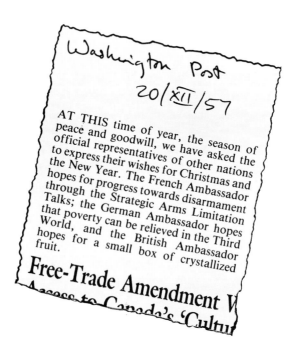

24 December 1957   *Sandringham House*

I'm getting very anxious about my first televised broadcast tomorrow. I spent the entire afternoon trying frocks on. Bobo says that I should wear a tiara because people expect it of me. It's very hard not to become irritable at times like this. If Margaret and the children sing 'Ding Dong Merrily on High' one more time I shall call the whole thing off.

The First Secretary of the Soviet Communist Party
The Kremlin
Moscow

19 December 1957

Your Imperial Majesty Elizabeth,

In a supreme effort to improve the relationship between our nations, I am sending you this little moralistic story, a favourite folktale of mine which I hope will be suitable for use in Your Majesty's Christmas broadcast.

One cold day in the Ukraine a small boy was walking through the woods, whistling. Suddenly he saw a small bird with a broken wing being chased by a hungry fox. The small boy picked up the bird, comforted it, and then looked for a warm and comfortable place where it could recover. At that moment, along came a horse and left a very large deposit in the middle of the road. The small boy scooped a hole in the deposit, put the small bird into it and went away, whistling.

The thoughtful boy was quite right. In the warm environment of the dung the little bird recovered, put out his head and sang. The hungry fox heard it, and ate the little bird.

The moral of this story is twofold: first, it is not always your enemies who put you in it, and secondly, if you are in it up to your neck, keep your mouth shut.

Nikita Khrushchev

Nikita Khrushchev

25 December 1957   *Sandringham House*

The dreaded day! First 90 technicians turned up, filling the drive with vans and frightening the corgis. In addition to the director and producer there were designers, make-up artists, furniture-removers, interior decorators, sound recordists and cameramen. No sooner had they arrived than they began to take up my carpet and lay down their own – one that had appeared in an *Arthur Haynes Show* sketch, it seems. They put in their own furniture and curtains too. I was speechless, but eventually it turned up in one of my handbags.

Electricians drilled holes through the walls to get the cables in, so when I finally did the broadcast such an icy gale was blowing round my legs that I shivered with cold rather than fright. Make-up girls dabbed bright yellow spots of make-up on my forehead, cheeks and nose (this is what they need for television, I gather). Then they gave me a black lipstick to put on. I think I shall buy Margaret one next Christmas – it would suit her better than it did me. By then I looked like something from *The Wizard of Oz!* Finally, Bobo zipped me into my latest Norman Hartnell, and Peter Dimmock (the producer) and Anthony Craxton (director) escorted me into the library as if I were a prisoner going to the death cell. The clapperboard clapped, cameras whirred, and the teleprompter began teleprompting. I looked at my library full of technicians, gazed into the camera and began: 'I welcome you to the peace of my home . . .'

Have I got to suffer this *every* year now? It seems I am destined never to enjoy another Christmas lunch.

1958

2 February 1958   *Buckingham Palace*
Had a meeting of new Privy councillors this afternoon, one of
the most hilarious I have ever attended. The new Councillors
have to line up in the anteroom while I stand in the White
Drawing Room with my hand on the table, as is required of
me. Then they come in, go down on one knee, take the Bible
in their right hand, advance three paces towards me, kiss my
hand and walk backwards ten paces without falling over the
stools that have been thoughtfully placed behind them. It can
take an hour to get through a dozen Privy Councillors if they
are ill-rehearsed, but today was a shambles. Somehow they got
in the wrong positions and were all crawling around on their
hands and knees hoping that I would not notice. Trying
desperately not to laugh, I kept saying the names of the corgis
over and over again in my mind to stop myself from giggling. I
heard Sir Edward Bridges say afterwards, 'Her Majesty must
have been furious – her face was like thunder.'
    If only he knew . . .

3 March 1958   *Buckingham Palace*
Charles has a tummy upset. Obviously the food at Hill House
School is too rich for him. He's not used to it at home.

3 July 1958   *Buckingham Palace*
The very last annual presentation of debutantes at court,
thank goodness. The final one was a Miss Fiona Macrae from
Edinburgh, so we had a nice chat about the Castle and the
Palace of Holyroodhouse. Five hundred debutantes have asked
if they can attend an informal luncheon.

4 July 1958   *Windsor Castle*
Watched Philip on television playing polo and looking very
dashing. If only I could have found something to criticize
about his playing: he always finds fault with *my* performances.
Saw ventriloquist Peter Brough on television too, with his

dummy Archie Andrews. Much better than on the wireless, where ventroloquists have about as much appeal as a juggling act.

26 July 1958   *Windsor Castle*
Have been feeling a bit under the weather today. Philip says it must be a germ from one of those frightful debutantes. Was unable to get to the British Empire and Commonwealth Games in Cardiff, and so that the Welsh don't think that it was a deliberate snub (they can be *so* sensitive) I have decided to make Charles Prince of Wales. Had great fun making a tape-recorded message, with Bobo working the tape-recorder while one of the Pages of the Backstairs (the one I like, with the Pat Boone hairstyle) held the microphone. The recording was played as a surprise at the closing of the games. Isn't modern technology marvellous! When we first played it back I thought that my voice sounded terribly high. Silly Bobo, she was playing it at the wrong speed – I think.

24 October 1958   *Buckingham Palace*
State Opening of Parliament. This is an ordeal at the best of times, as I have to balance a $2\frac{1}{2}$-lb crown on my head whilst reading the current prime minister's speech. This year we had the added intrusion of television cameras. Am I to be dogged by these *everywhere* I go? I'm already getting butterflies about my Christmas broadcast and it's two months away yet. Now people are laughing at my phrase 'My husband and I'. What on earth is so funny about that, and how else am I supposed to refer to us both?

5 December 1958   *Buckingham Palace*
Inaugurated Britain's STD telephone service in Bristol today by dialling directly to the Lord Provost of Edinburgh, Ian Johnson-Gilbert. The number appeared to be unobtainable, but eventually the operator managed to get it for me.

WINDSOR CASTLE

My husband and I

I and my husband

Me and my husband } *grammar?*

We - he and I -

Philip and I

I and Philip } *too informal*

The Duke of Edinburgh and myself   *too formal*

The Prince and I   *sounds like a Rodgers & Hammerstein musical!*

I, as the Queen, and my husband   *too wordy*

My spouse and I

I and my better half   *no - that would further inflate his ego*

The old man and me   *too common*

Charles and Anne's father and I

My beloved and I   *no - sounds like Queen Victoria*

The father of my children and I

Both of us

My little Philly-poos and I

The man I married and I

Remember my wedding in Westminster Abbey in 1947? Well, that fellow
   who stood beside me, he and I...   *too long-winded*

The Duke and I

I and the Duke

Mr Mountbatten and I

Mr Windsor and I   *Philip wouldn't like that at all!*

My husband and I   *Yes! That's a good one. I like it.*

1959

8 *January 1959*   *Sandringham House*

The President of France, General de Gaulle, was officially installed today. Members of the Cabinet wanted me to send a good luck telegram, but France is a republic, so I didn't. I only send telegrams if there is a national disaster. According to Philip, de Gaulle *is* a national disaster.

Margaret suggested that the Buckingham Palace Brownie Pack (the B'hams) should be re-formed to provide an interest for Anne now that she is eight. I know that we had great fun in our childhood, learning how to rub sticks together, identify real pearls from fakes, diamonds from paste, paint copies of Rembrandt's pictures, and what to do with a toggle (or was it a woggle?). In fact it is a good training for life. So I agreed. The Brownie Pack will also give Anne an opportunity to mix with some ordinary girls, like Sukie Babington-Smith, grand-daughter of Admiral the Honourable Sir Herbert Meade-Featherstonehaugh, and Caroline Hamilton, the Dean of Windsor's grandchild. They can pitch their tents in Windsor Great Park while the Castle's kitchen staff cook beans and sausages for them and run them over there by jeep. Anne is very excited.

26 *January 1959*   *Buckingham Palace*

Michael Adeane tells me that the sentries outside the Palace are revolting. They are to go on strike because they are fed up with suffering the indignities inflicted upon them by hordes of tourists attempting to destroy their composure. I must say I agree with them. It must be very difficult to retain a straight face when you are being taunted by crowds of strangers. I actually heard one woman shout to a mounted sentry, 'Can I stroke what's between your legs?' I think she meant the horse – but I couldn't be certain. I have told them that they can move the sentry boxes off the pavement into the Palace forecourt behind the railings.

Margaret seems to have taken up with a nice young man, albeit a commoner, with the surname of Jones.

1 March 1959   *Windsor Castle*

Vicious attacks on my relevance to the country today in many newspapers. Do I play an important role or am I merely an anachronism?, MPs are asking. I telephoned Mr Macmillan (I *still* cannot bring myself to call him Harold. He seems so grandfatherly that somehow it seems too familiar. In many ways he seems older than Churchill.) He says that I should always ignore the Sunday papers.

'But Prime Minister, they're saying I'm not needed any more,' I explained.

'They don't know when they're well off. They've never had it so good,' he scoffed.

Decided to change the Trooping of the Colour ceremony from Thursday to Saturday. That will stop complaints about its causing traffic congestion. Maybe I should have a Jubilee or something to drum up some patriotism.

4 March 1959   *Buckingham Palace*

Was just exercising my horse in the Palace gardens this morning when Philip bawled something at me from the Bow Room. I thought either Britain had been declared a republic or he'd managed to lose his polo mallet again. I was just about to shout that Anne had borrowed it for putting up a tent when I saw that he had a gentleman with him. It turned out to be a Mr Bernard Goldberg, the director of a public relations company and part-time Hollywood film producer. Philip had called him in to see how the image of the royal family could be improved.

We went into the Belgian Suite for coffee.

'Now *this* room could be brightened up for a start,' he said, before presenting us with a number of ideas. Among them were:

1.   I should change my hair colour and sack my dressmakers.
2.   If I were to become pregnant within the next year it would make the public more sympathetic to us, knowing that we now have a larger family to support.
3.   A royal wedding would be good for morale. Could I get

either Margaret, Alexandra or the Duke of Kent married off, or at the very least announce whom Anne will eventually marry?
4. Buckingham Palace should be opened up as a health and leisure centre.
5. Philip and I should make a record, for example with the Everly Brothers, in time for Christmas, or, failing that, with Conway Twitty.
6. I should be interviewed by Noele Gordon on *Lunch Box*.

Shall we make it through the 'sixties?

6 June 1959   *Buckingham Palace*
Trooped the Colour. It's all very well having it on a Saturday, but it shortens my weekend. Nearly missed this afternoon's racing. Bobo is packing for our Canadian tour.

9 June 1959   *Buckingham Palace*
Felt very sick this morning. Don't know how I got through the investiture. Made one woman a dame who had only come to see her husband get an MBE.

17 June 1959   *Buckingham Palace*
Discovered that I am expecting a little prince or princess in the New Year. It came as such a shock. If I hadn't had what I thought was indigestion I would never have called in the Physician to the Household. I just wanted to be able to enjoy this evening's farewell dinner. My condition is to be kept secret until we get back from my Canadian tour. Among the documents in the dispatch box this evening was a report that the population of the world is now 2800 million, and increasing at a rate of 45 million a year: has somebody already leaked the news of my pregnancy to the government? I can't trust anybody nowadays.

6 July 1959   *The White House, Washington DC*
A flying visit to Washington. I am finding this whole tour very exacting. The morning sickness seems to be worse than it was

with Charles or Anne, and it's all the more difficult because nobody knows. Philip says that I should carry a very large handbag with me in the mornings, but I really don't think that's the answer. I was having a quiet drink with Mamie Eisenhower this afternoon and thought it would do no harm to tell her.

'Gee, that's wonderful! Have a large martini!' she cried, obviously excited by my news.

'But it must be kept a total secret, Mamie,' I pleaded. 'You're to tell nobody.'

'You can trust me, honey!' she roared, then shouted to the President, 'Say, Ike, Lizzie's pregnant. Isn't that marvellous!'

'Well, you can just tell Mr Eisenhower,' I murmured into my martini.

18 July 1959   *Montreal, Canada*
Philip and I were invited to a ball here this evening in our honour. When we arrived the place was so crowded with people wanting to see us – they were even standing on the tables – that we were the only people who couldn't get in. I was so disappointed.

Next time there is a function in our honour perhaps nobody should be told we are coming, then the problem couldn't arise.

Instead we had a rare opportunity to watch real Canadian television – a documentary about Noël Coward and a 1933 Gracie Fields film.

8 October 1959   *Buckingham Palace*
Having no engagements I was able to watch the General Election on television today. We don't know the result yet, but it looks certain that Mr Macmillan will be returned with a large majority. He'll be so pleased – he's only just had the drawing-room at Number 10 redecorated.

1960

19 February 1960   *Buckingham Palace*

Gave birth to a baby prince at 3.30 p.m. This was certainly the easiest labour I've had, though it will always be the most difficult situation in which to retain any semblance of dignity. The nurses wore sterilized paper bags while the gynaecologist spent most of his time with his head under the candlewick bedspread, so that no one could actually see anything. Philip spent the day playing squash and swimming: it was a very worrying time for him.

A visit from Mummy this evening, and also Margaret, with Anthony Jones, her fiancé. He's going to add the prefix 'Armstrong' to his surname so he doesn't sound too working-class. I shall have to ennoble him, I suppose, so that Margaret isn't just Mrs Armstrong-Jones. Spent the evening quietly examining government papers, including Wolfenden's recommendations on homosexuality.

20 February 1960   *Buckingham Palace*

Decided to call our new prince 'Andrew' after my father-in-law. I wanted to call him Edward, after Great-Great-Grandfather, but Philip pointed out that we already have an 'Eddie' with the Duke of Kent, so we're using it as a middle name instead. Some confusion seems to have arisen over our surname – to which no one gave a second thought when we were married. Are we Windsors or Mountbattens? If I say we're Windsors, Philip will have to change his name. If we're not, then I change history and we become 'The House of Mountbatten'.

Charles and Anne came to see me for ten minutes today, just so that they don't feel pushed out (or down, in Anne's case), and I explained the dilemma to them.

'Why don't we become Mountbatten-Windsors?' asked Anne. So we have.

Children see things so logically, don't they?

2 May 1960   *Windsor Castle*
Tonight I held a reception for all the heads of state who are
over here for the Commonwealth Conference. I have to tread
very carefully so that I don't appear to be spending more time
with the Prime Minister of one country than another. This
means I'm swept amongst them rather like a dessert trolley.
My fleeting impressions were of an Anglo-Indian colonel
(Ayub of Pakistan); a bag of nerves (Diefenbaker of Canada)
and an ultra-royalist (Menzies of Australia). But one advantage
of this type of function is that I get invited to visit all their
countries. I've enough state visits lined up now for the next
decade.

6 May 1960   *Buckingham Palace*
Margaret's wedding day. I was delighted to see the Abbey so
full considering that an unprecedented number of wedding
invitations were turned down. We invited the 15th/19th
regiment of the King's Hussars, of which she is Colonel-in-
Chief, and the Women's Royal Australian Army Corps to
make up the numbers, and luckily we had been able to track
down Tony's father (on honeymoon in Bermuda with the
third Mrs Armstrong-Jones senior). I must say that my darling
sister looked lovely in her Hartnell gown, topped by the
Poltimore tiara. It's lucky too that Tony is so short because
they make the perfect couple.
    'I've quite forgotten about Peter,' she mouthed to me just
before kneeling at the altar.
    They had some lovely presents, including a plot of building
land in Mustique from Colin Tennant, which was extremely
generous of him. Margaret and Tony are going to have a little
villa built there.

9 December 1960   *Buckingham Palace*
A fascinating new television serial called *Coronation Street*
started this evening. I thought at first that it was something to
do with London SW1, but in fact it's about life amongst the
working classes in the north of England, and it gives a

marvellous insight into how other people live. I'm fascinated by the idea of 'milk stout'. I would never have imagined beer and milk together could make an acceptable drink.

They say the serial is scheduled to run for 26 weeks, so I won't be able to watch all of it.

Charles comes home from school tomorrow for the Christmas holidays.

Andrew said his first word today: 'Corgi.'

10 December 1960   *Buckingham Palace*

Charles came home with a cardboard crown that he had made for his school nativity play: strange, really – he was playing a shepherd. I wish I could have seen the play, but I was launching a Royal Navy nuclear submarine at the time.

Eddie, Duke of Kent, visited us for dinner this evening with his fiancée, Miss Katherine Worsley. She's a shop assistant, I think, but the daughter of Sir William Worsley, and *such* a dignified girl. She'll make a marvellous duchess. Unfortunately Princess Marina is already Duchess of Kent, so next year we'll have two.

Margaret rang up in tears. She and Tony had had an argument. It was all over nothing, I think – he refused to address her as 'Ma'am' in public. I do think they should have sorted all this out long ago. How can you get married without knowing what you're going to be called in future?

CHEAM PREPARATORY SCHOOL

End of Term Report ....Autumn.....19.60

PUPIL..HRH THE PRINCE CHARLES.......... FORM....III A.....

DATE OF BIRTH...14 November 1948......... FORM MASTER..H.G.........

Subject	Examination results %	Master's comments
MATHEMATICS	10	Little interest — claims Keeper of Privy Purse and Chancellor of Exchequer will handle his sums. F.M.
ENGLISH LANGUAGE	65	Improving — but is confused about personal pronouns. Refers to himself as "one". End-of-term composition "The Young Boy of Lochnagar" vastly better than last term's "The Middle-aged Woman of Lochnagar". T.W.
ENGLISH LITERATURE	97	A joy to teach — and always a mint-condition first edition of every book we study! D.M.
LATIN	—	Shows little interest — has opted for a private course in Welsh instead. R.G.
HISTORY	76	Excellent. Difficult to fault on Kings and Queens of England, though a bit vague about Oliver Cromwell. A.M.G.
GEOGRAPHY	87	A lively interest in all Commonwealth countries. T.V.
RELIGIOUS KNOWLEDGE	56	Promising, but constantly tries to pull rank on grounds that he's related to the Head of the Church. G.
CHEMISTRY	2	Little aptitude for science. Has yet to master intricacies of bunsen burner. J.C.
BIOLOGY	52	Above average but increasingly obsessed with carbuncles and tends to talk to plants. H.E.
ART	—	Studies of wildlife and old men are exceptional — thanks to father's tuition perhaps? J.H.
MUSIC	—	He has been persuaded to give up the trumpet this term and will be savaging the cello now he has grown a little. J.P.
SPORT	—	Enjoys board games and watching polo, but not a strong rugby player. Expect better from future Prince of Wales. N.M.

MATRON'S REPORT Always a little depressed for first eight weeks of term. Won't let me give him a proper medical. Doesn't wash behind ears. Should undergo treatment for the arm, presumably deformed, that he always hides behind his back. C.M.

HEADMASTER'S REPORT This boy is a real asset to the school and should in due course be appointed Head Boy. It would be preferable if his parents could attend more school functions and take an active role in the Parent-Teachers Association. It would also be good for his morale if he could have a new uniform: his is the most threadbare in the school and still bears the old badge we stopped using in 1949. (Name tape in blazer says "Philip Mountbatten".)
 Charles is a quiet boy with few friends other than his personal detective. I would not advise that he join the Cadets — he is not Forces material. But he has the makings of a librarian or a priest and should give his career some thought before too long if he is to avoid unemployment on leaving school.
 T. Macpherson

The.....SPRING....... term will begin on.....7 JANUARY 1961..............

1961

30 June 1961   *Windsor Castle*

Philip broke an ankle bone on the Cowdray Polo Field and now he's hobbling about with his foot in plaster. Mummy also cracked a bone in her foot, at Royal Lodge, so I have two invalids on my hands. Couldn't help laughing as the cripples hobbled in for tea. It's so nice to have a rest after the hustle and bustle of the Kents' wedding.

'I'm really enjoying the break,' I remarked, without thinking. The cripples scowled at me across the tea-table.

3 November 1961   *Buckingham Palace*

Margaret and Tony are still squabbling about who should sit at the head of the table. I've decided to make him an earl, which will sort things out once and for all. Their first baby is due in a month's time and we can't have him growing up as plain Jones, albeit with an Armstrong in front of it.

Mr Macmillan is trying to put a stop to my forthcoming tour of Ghana because there have been threats on the life of President Nkrumah and one or two bomb explosions. Even Sir Anthony Eden and Winston Churchill have put their spokes in – but Bobo has packed for the tour now, and she'll be in such a bad mood if I ask her to unpack. So I've decided to go. I'll send my Commonwealth Secretary there first and if he returns unscathed all should be well. How silly I would look if I were to cancel and Khruschev were to go and have a good reception.

10 November 1961   *Ambassadors Hotel, Accra, Ghana*

We finally reached Ghana, after being delayed by fog at London airport for five hours. We sat in the VIP Lounge playing 'spot the double-take' – counting the number of unsuspecting people who see me and cannot believe their eyes.

Philip got impatient and shouted at a few people, but I pretended not to hear. I called for some of the red boxes and studied the papers proposing Britain's entry into the Common

Market, for which negotiations began in Brussels today. We eventually arrived in Ghana at 9 o'clock instead of teatime, which made my procession through the streets in an open-topped car a bit pointless as there were no streetlights. People lit the occasional match or shone torches in my face so that they could see me. I just waved and smiled. Nobody threw anything at me, so I think we should be all right. Margaret is to call her new baby 'David', after the Duke of Windsor. Philip says it's typical of her to name him after the black sheep of the family.

14 November 1961   *Ambassadors Hotel, Accra, Ghana*
Charles' thirteenth birthday and once more I am away from home. I seem to miss all my family's celebrations. We have given him some ear muffs (extra large) and a formal photograph (framed) of ourselves just in case he forgets what his mother and father look like. Philip also arranged for him to have a course of lessons with the Household Brigade Polo Club. Perhaps that's why he was so delighted when Andrew was born – if we keep going we can have our own polo team. Kwame Nkrumah seems to enjoy his role as President here. Every time we go out together he has the crowds whipped up into a frenzy, all shouting, '*Osayfo* is coming!' ('*Osayfo*' is the Ghanaian word for Messiah, I've learned). As Head of the Church of England and Defender of the Faith, I found this intolerable, so I had Michael Adeane put a stop to it. I told Nkrumah that the shouting was hurting my ears, so as not to offend him.

20 November 1961   *Berending, The Gambia*
Our fourteenth wedding anniversary and how I miss not spending it at Luton Hoo as we always have previously. The people here are very kind and have given us a 2-year-old crocodile in a pierced silver biscuit box as a present for Prince Andrew. It was very thoughtful of them, but I haven't the faintest idea what to do with it. We have put it in my Private Secretary's bath, but how we shall get it through customs I don't know. One of my equerries said that the crocodile snaps

less than my corgis. Obviously their training has worked!

Was informed by telegram that my Government has accepted the principle of decimal coinage. I'm not sure that I agree. One hundred pence to the pound instead of 240 seems a dramatic drop to me. I'm so glad that I don't ever have to carry money.

30 December 1961　　　　　　　*Sandringham House*
It snowed. We all played charades to keep warm.

1962

2 January 1962　　　　　　　*Sandringham House*
More snow. Spent the day in my room doing the boxes and a jigsaw.

7 January 1962　　　　　　　*Sandringham House*
Even more snow. Watched a film in the ballroom, an Alfred Hitchcock thriller as the children like them. This one was called *Psycho*. Cancelled my plans to have showers installed here.

18 March 1962　　　　　　　*Buckingham Palace*
Charles was admonished in the press by the Lord's Day Observance Society for skiing on the Sabbath. I told him not to worry. The same thing happened to me when I went racing at Longchamps with the President of France on a Sunday. I shall make a point of having him well scrubbed and travelling in the same car as myself when we go to church at Easter. And I must try to stop him doing Goon impressions when photographers are around.

12 April 1962　　　　　　　*Windsor Castle*
The press is speculating that Charles will marry Princess Caroline of Monaco. The poor boy's only 13. He says that he

doesn't want to marry until he's 30. Now we'll have 17 years of speculation, I suppose.

Margaret and Tony arguing over who should have the larger Easter egg.

30 August 1962   *Balmoral Castle*
Charles was criticized in the press by the anti-blood sports people because he went on the annual stag shoot. I shall try to get him to attend a World Wildlife fund-raising function.

12 October 1962   *Buckingham Palace*
Charles got into a spot of bother on a school outing to Stornoway. At an hotel appropriately called 'The Crown' he found himself hounded by people pressing their noses against the window to get a closer look at him. (The same thing happened to me only last week on a visit to Huddersfield.) In an effort to get away from them he fled into the bar and ordered a cherry brandy. Inevitably, a journalist was standing next to him and there was his story – a 14-year-old prince drinking alcohol in public. I was so embarrassed. Nobody drinks cherry brandy at lunchtime.

Poor little Charles. I shall see if I can get him the presidency of Alcoholics Anonymous when he's older.

1963

7 January 1963   *Sandringham House*

What a winter! I've never known anything like it. Philip says it must be a new Ice Age. All the lavatories here are frozen up so we all have to troop out and use the old facilities behind the stables. Thank goodness it's too cold for photographers to hang around.

Persuaded my horse trainer, Captain Moore, to retire. He's 81 and his methods are at times a little bit dated. I'm going to give him a grace-and-favour home at Hampton Court, so he'll still be able to potter about the stud. I don't think he wanted to retire, and when I asked him how he was feeling he said, 'Well, ma'am, I feel like a rabbit who has been bolted by a ferret.'

I may have been called many things behind my back, but never a ferret to my face!

21 September 1963   *Balmoral Castle*

Anne seems to have settled in well at Benenden. Her dorm is called 'Magnolia' – my least favourite colour.

She sent me a note saying that she is to be a mother, which was somewhat perturbing as she's still only 13. I immediately rang her headmistress, Miss Clarke. It turns out she means a house mother, looking after some other girls. What a relief – we're having enough problems with Charles.

Dr Middleton has confirmed, however, that *I* am to be a mother again.

'Soon have the whole polo team,' commented Philip when I told him. I shall cancel all my engagements after we return from Balmoral. Mummy, Margaret and the Princess Royal can undertake my duties. Ordered ten new jigsaws. Bobo is already unpacking my maternity smocks.

18 October 1963   *Buckingham Palace*

Harold Macmillan has resigned as PM due to ill health. I returned from Balmoral to a barrage of telegrams from people wanting the position: Quentin Hogg (no, he'd have to renounce his peerage and I couldn't possibly have Prime Minister Hogg!), Selwyn Lloyd (do we really want a Welshman in the job, I wonder?), dear Rab Butler ('Please, Ma'am,' he writes, 'I'm *always* the bridesmaid, never the bride!'), Maudling, Heath, Macleod, Thorneycroft . . . it's incredible. If only the premiership could be hereditary like the royal family we would have none of this.

19 October 1963   *Buckingham Palace*
Visited Mr Macmillan in hospital. He was on the bedpan when I arrived.

   'No, please don't get up,' I said.

   'QUEEN TO SEND FOR BUTLER TODAY,' said *The Times'* headline, which at first struck me as odd – after all, I send for butlers every day of my life.

   However, I sent for Lord Home, one of the few people who has not tried to push for leadership. He is even prepared to renounce his peerage and become plain Sir Alec Douglas-Home.

5 November 1963   *Buckingham Palace*
Sir Alec came for his first weekly audience. He is a very genteel man and seems quite shy. I made a joke, in view of the date, saying that I hoped there wasn't a twentieth-century Guy Fawkes in Parliament today. He smiled, but I don't think he really understood. He's *very* English and apparently used to play cricket for Middlesex: that will please Philip, as he likes a sporting man. But Sir Alec doesn't seem too interested in racing, so we got straight down to business and discussed the Anglo-French report recommending a Channel tunnel, the Denning report on the Profumo affair and the Robbins report on higher education. I tried to catch him out once or twice, but he's done his homework, which is good.

   Bobo swung a watch over my tummy and says that I am going to have a princess.

THE
GEORGE GERSHWIN
APPRECIATION SOCIETY

411 RHAPSODY HOUSE, 837 THIRD AVENUE, NEW YORK, NY 10022

30 December 1963

Your Majesty,

As I am sure that Your Majesty is aware, 26 September 1998 will mark the centenary of the birth of our great composer George Gershwin.

Knowing how early your engagement calendar gets full, we thought we would contact you well in advance to ask Your Majesty to honor us with a visit on this date in 1998, when we hope to stage a special performance in your honor of a newly discovered Gershwin musical entitled Corgi and Beth.

We at the George Gershwin Appreciation Society sincerely hope that it will be possible for Your Majesty to attend.

Your obedient servant,

Larry P. Cornelius
President.

Decline this one. It's a Saturday and I'll be at the annual Ghillies' Ball at Balmoral.
ER

1964

1 January 1964   *Sandringham House*
Margaret, Princess Alexandra, the Duchess of Kent and I are
all awaiting happy events in the next few months. Philip says
that Sandringham looks more like an ante-natal clinic than a
country house. Certainly there are problems when we all meet
in the corridor. I am so relieved that I had the foresight to
record my Christmas broadcast last September, otherwise I
would have filled the screen. It took three footmen to get me
into the car when we went to church, and the Bishop had to
help release me at the other end.

15 March 1964   *Buckingham Palace*
The Belgian Suite suddenly became a delivery room when my
waters broke in the middle of a private audience. Fortunately
this was with my gynaecologist, so it was not a wasted journey
for him. A baby prince was born at 8.20 p.m. this evening,
which meant that I had to keep Sir Alec waiting a little for his
Tuesday audience, but he kindly said that he had nothing else
planned anyway. People still don't seem to recognize him in
the streets and he gets very few evening invitations. In fact a
surprising number of people are still unaware that he *is* Prime
Minister.

   We are going to call the baby 'Edward'; if he did ever
become king he would be Edward IX – quite an achievement,
as we've never had more than eight of any name yet.

10 April 1964   *Windsor Castle*
Harold Macmillan declined the earldom I offered him, and the
Order of the Garter. I wondered if it was because we didn't
make him godfather to Edward, but Philip claims that
Macmillan thinks he's *the* Godfather anyway.

16 October 1964   *Buckingham Palace*
Poor Sir Alec lost the General Election – and he's hardly been
PM five minutes. I think he's too much of a gentleman to be in
politics. The electorate only respects politicians it can't trust.

Harold Wilson won by a very tiny majority. He came to the Palace this afternoon to 'kiss hands'. He grabbed hold of my arm and practically devoured my hand, covering it in kisses. I snatched it away (he still had his pipe in his mouth) and told him that the kissing should be taken as read. Not only is he now head of a Labour government, but he comes from Huddersfield. There'll be pigeons in the garden of Number 10 before we know it. He was not wearing morning dress and he arrived with his wife, his sister and his father in tow as if I were the Ideal Home exhibition. I had been doing the boxes very thoroughly, so I asked him exactly what he intended to do about the £800 million balance of payments deficit. He was like a schoolboy who hadn't done his homework!

'I didn't think we'd discuss things like that on my first day,' he said. 'I wondered if you have any good tips for the 3.30 at Doncaster?'

1965

20 May 1965   *Schloss Bruhl, Berlin*
Third day of our visit to West Germany, where we have been very well received. They have even composed a Queen Elizabeth Foxtrot in my honour, which Philip and I have been practising in the bedroom. I got mixed up in the pre-election war here, which was actually quite amusing. Willy Brandt, the Mayor of Berlin, is also leader of the Social Democrats and is challenging Chancellor Erhard. *Both* men felt that they should sit beside me in the car, which led to such a heated argument that they ended up not speaking to each other. I suggested a compromise. Both sat facing me on the little tip-up seats, with their backs to the driver. I gave them one of my frosty looks and waved to the people on the route. One disconcerting moment as I stood on a balcony and faced throngs of people, all shouting, 'Elizabet! Elizabet!' For one fleeting moment it sounded as if they were chanting '*Sieg Heil!*'

22 December 1965   *Buckingham Palace*

A meeting this evening to discuss Charles' future as he has just turned 17. The Prime Minister, the Archbishop of Canterbury, Earl Mountbatten and the Chairman of the Committee of University Vice-Chancellors came here for dinner. After much discussion it was decided that he will go to Trinity College, Cambridge, like Daddy; Dartmouth like Daddy and Philip, and then to sea with the Royal Navy, perhaps with a command of his own, by which time he should be married and ready to embark on the round of royal duties. I felt relieved that his future now seems secure. Harold Wilson had the effrontery to suggest that I abdicate when Charles reaches 21, so that we don't have 'an Edward VII situation'.

'And if I abdicate we'll have an Edward VIII situation!' I said through gritted teeth, picking up my handbag to indicate that the meeting was at an end.

Sad to hear that dear Richard Dimbleby died today. Now there will be nobody to commentate at weddings and coronations.

1966

31 July 1966   *Windsor Castle*

Princess Alexandra gave birth to a daughter, whom they are going to call 'Marina' after her mother. There are now five babies in the family – it will be nothing but nappies this summer at Balmoral.

The King and Queen of Thailand called on me unexpectedly this afternoon. Philip was playing polo at Smith's Lawn, Mummy was having a nap at Royal Lodge and Margaret and Tony had taken all the children on a picnic in Windsor Great Park. I was just soaking my feet in a bowl of water, while looking through some correspondence (a letter from Mary Quant asking if I would accept the gift of a mini-skirt: who *does* she think I am?), when I noticed a carriage procession coming up the drive. As it was Sunday I had only one page and my personal footman, Roy, here with me. I quickly put on some shoes and a hat and sat in the Red Drawing Room as if I were expecting them. Fortunately neither of them speaks English, so I didn't have to make conversation. We sang each other's national anthem instead, and I gave them both a Grand Cross of the Royal Victorian Order while the boys managed to find some Lapsang Souchong and a few noodles. It seemed to keep them happy, but it was a bit of an ordeal. I am having a short guide to British royal etiquette translated into Thai for them. Rule no. 1: we do not call on monarchs unannounced.

Mummy has had a 'blower' installed at Clarence House, which saves her having to keep sending someone to the betting shop.

29 August 1966   *Balmoral Castle*
Charles has passed two A-levels. Together with the five O-levels he already has they should get him to Cambridge without our having to suppress his results. I'm so thrilled for him – his future prospects are now much improved.

1967

9 March 1967   *Windsor Castle*
'Hemlines a neat four inches above the knee,' say the fashion magazines.

Not mine! Got Bobo to turn my hems up half-an-inch as a concession, then they can be let down again when the fashion changes.

29 March 1967   *Normandy*
One of my rare private visits to France, this time with Lord Porchester, who is now in charge of my horses, his wife and Michael Adeane: a nice little foursome. What sheer luxury it is

to do nothing but look at horses. I have already purchased two marvellous stallions. As we go about Normandy a lot of old men raise their berets and shout, '*Vive la Duchesse!*' Well, I *am* descended from the Dukes of Normandy, so they're not far from the truth.

President de Gaulle tried to send me some flowers, but when he rang Interflora and announced that the President of France wanted to send roses to the Queen of England, the assistant said, '*Oui, et moi je suis Jeanne d'Arc!*' (or words to that effect).

20 September 1967   *Balmoral Castle*

Received a note from Charles today. He is enjoying life at Trinity College but says he needs more money. He should learn from Anne. She gets £1 a term at Benenden and still comes home with change. Mummy says that if she used it wisely she should come back with a profit. Charles wants to join the Labour Party in Cambridge, but I will have to put my foot down there. As a future king he should not involve himself with trifles.

23 September 1967   *Balmoral Castle*

Harold and Mrs Wilson are here with us for the weekend, which has been an experience. They kindly gave us a bottle of Wincarnis when they arrived, which I assume must be a working-class wine. We had a small dinner party this evening with some of the local people from the estate and the local vicar. While he and Mrs Wilson were discussing the world's problems, the vicar pointed heavenwards and said, 'There is one above who knows the answer to everything.'

'Yes,' said Mary, 'Harold will be down in a minute. He's having problems with his evening suit.'

I spluttered into my sherry. When Harold did emerge he was wearing one of Philip's old kilts in the Balmoral tartan.

'I hadn't realized it was fancy dress,' said Margaret, loudly.

When we went in to dinner Mary produced a bottle of HP Sauce from her handbag and placed it before Harold: it seems she does this at every mealtime.

24 September 1967　　　　　　　*Balmoral Castle*

Was almost late for church this morning after a very late night listening to Margaret and the PM singing around the piano until 2 a.m. We had to send an equerry down to Ballater off-licence to buy some Guinness for them. (Mummy told me later that she had a crate at Birkhall we could have used.) Harold is actually quite fun after a couple of glasses and does a very good impersonation of Harold Macmillan doing the 'Wind of Change' speech. He then sang a couple of choruses of 'Her Name Was Mary', which was followed by Margaret's parody of Gertrude Lawrence singing 'Some Day I'll Find You'. I do hope she wasn't thinking of Peter Townsend again.

Found an envelope under our bedroom door in Mary Wilson's handwriting . . .

BALMORAL CASTLE

Ode to Balmoral
by Mary Wilson

Up to Balmoral we have been
To spend the weekend with our Queen.
Harold dressed up in raincoat smart,
He's the PM and looks the part.
Princess Margaret was there,
The Queen Mum too,
With her silver hair
And jewels, like dew.
We've had some fun,
We've played some games;
There's been no sun,
Like the Queen, it rains.
As with all good things
The end has come,
So we bid farewell
And thank you, Ma'am.

Now that John Masefield's passed away, I suppose you're looking for a new Poet Laureate, aren't you?
M.W.

What a blessing I have already decided upon Cecil Day-Lewis. Maybe we can get Mary on to *Opportunity Knocks* instead.

1968

10 June 1968   *Windsor Castle*

Installed Charles as a Knight of the Garter, which provided him with a good rehearsal for next year's investiture.

Audience with the PM. He has finally talked me into allowing a film crew to follow us around for an entire year in 1969. Harold is convinced it will be a valuable public relations exercise, and Philip thinks it will bring the royal family right into the 1970s. I have my reservations, though. They want to show that we are human beings but I can't help thinking of Bagehot's words about letting 'daylight in upon magic'. Does the public really want to see us doing *ordinary* things like choosing the luncheon menu, selecting which tiara to wear, collecting our hot-water bottles ready for the carriage drive to Parliament and greeting the hordes at a garden party? I've had to make some provisos, however, to maintain some degree of dignity and decorum:

1. I am not to be filmed under the hairdrier.
2. Charles is not to be filmed from the back – he looks like a Rolls-Royce with the doors open.
3. Margaret and Tony must not appear.
4. Mummy may appear only if she doesn't speak.
5. Anne may speak as long as it's in French.
6. If Philip swears the words must be bleeped out.
7. No audience with Harold Wilson is to be filmed. It would be inadvisable for anyone to know what we really talk about.
8. Only the best rooms at Buckingham Palace may be shown.

9.   It is not to be revealed that I only have two handbags, nor is Bobo to be filmed while she's painting either of them with shoe dye.
10.   There are to be as many shots of horses and dogs as possible. That's what people expect.

1969

7 March 1969   *Buckingham Palace*

Opened the Victoria Line Underground, which was a novel experience. Bobo insisted that I wear a thermal vest, a fur coat and a miner's helmet – she doesn't understand modern transport.

We started at Green Park, as that's one of our nearest tube stations, and met the Lieutenant of Greater London, the Mayor, the Chairman of the Council, the Minister of Transport, the Commissioner of Police, our local MP and so on. Went down an escalator – where I met nine more people – then to a ticket hall, where I was introduced to eleven more. I was handed a sixpenny piece to put in the ticket machine, to make it look as if I were paying for my journey (that seemed to make the photographers very happy), but when I put it in the slot it was instantly rejected. We tried four different coins before I could get a ticket, by which time I'd virtually given up hope of ever seeing a train – thank heavens I'm not a commuter.

We then had a very smooth ride to Oxford Circus, where I met more people and made a speech in which I observed that as they had been digging under the Mall to construct the Underground I have a vested interest in it. Eventually we travelled to Victoria, where I had to pay excess fare as apparently my ticket was only valid for Oxford Circus.

14 May 1969   *Crabtree Hall, Yorkshire*

It's getting rather tiresome to have a film crew constantly trailing us. They've been pointing their intrusive lenses at me for 11 months now and at times I'm tempted to stick out my tongue and thumb my nose at them. I get into a carriage and they're there; I drive my car at Windsor and there's a man lying on the bonnet shining a light in my face. We have picnics and barbeques set up for them to film, then go inside and have a proper lunch when they've finished filming and are having a break in the local hostelry. This evening we went to dinner with Lord and Lady Crabtree, and sure enough the cameras followed us. Fortunately Lady Constance, who is very practical, contrived to lock the entire crew in her bedroom until after the meal. As this room was once a mausoleum this seemed to be eminently appropriate.

By the time they'd finished filming it was very late and we ended up staying the night, which also gave us a few hours' respite from the film crew.

'I'll have to hang a sign saying "Queen Elizabeth slept here" over the bed,' said Lady Constance, laughing.

Over my dead body.

Telephoned Bobo and told her not to wait up with the cocoa, and to take the corgis out.

24 June 1969   *Windsor Castle*

Our film was shown on television this evening. I was rather nervous about it as Mr Cawston, its director, had refused to let us see the finished film before the broadcast. A whole year's filming and the entire programme lasted less than two hours! Philip said afterwards that it was 'a bloody pointless exercise, showing us doing silly things that we never normally do' – a total reversal of his earlier attitude to the project.

Afterwards we received a telephone call from Lew Grade asking whether he could turn it into a musical.

I thought the children came across very well, but Bobo has become rather carried away by her moments of television exposure. She refuses to eat with the rest of the staff now.

25 June 1969   *Buckingham Palace*
Decided not to make a Christmas broadcast this year. They
can show the *Royal Family* film instead, which will bring us in
repeat fees. Presented new colours to the 2nd Battalion
Grenadier Guards and attended a garden party. Quite missed
the cameramen being around. There seems to be a gap in my
life now.

1 July 1969   *Caernarvon Castle, Wales*
Charles' investiture as Prince of Wales – a very exciting day.
Lord Snowdon had designed a very futuristic-looking platform
for the ceremony and a very strange uniform for himself:
bottle green with a zip-front and a tasselled belt. The Duke of
Norfolk remarked that all he needed was a hat with a feather
in it and he could pass for Robin Hood.

The ceremony nearly had to take place without me as the
royal train was held up at Crewe; then when we got to
Caernarvon there weren't enough cars. The Kents ended up
travelling in a vegetable van, and when Margaret arrived at
the Castle they wouldn't let her in at first because she didn't
have a security pass. This was all very stressful, and poor
Margaret was so upset that she had to keep excusing herself
throughout the ceremony, which was awfully disconcerting.
But the moment I most feared came when I had to put the
crown on Charles' head: I had this vision of it going right over
his eyes, but fortunately his ears held it in place. God has a
reason for everything, it seems.

However, we have decided that if Anne, Andrew or Edward
acquire any extra titles there will be no more investitures of
this sort.

21 July 1969   *Buckingham Palace*
Neil Armstrong and Edwin Aldrin became the first men to
walk on the moon. What a nice gesture to make for Charles'
investiture year. Harold and Mary Wilson came to watch it on
our television. Surely they weren't worried about their
electricity bill?

BUCKINGHAM PALACE

My Lords and Members of the House of Commons, my husband and I look forward with pleasure to our visits to Brazil, Jamaica, Hong Kong, New Zealand, Australia, Japan, Mexico, the Bahamas and anywhere else we can find to go. As my family has been seen with such frequency on television in the last few months we will not be undertaking any engagements in 1970 for fear of over-exposure, knowing full well that you can have too much of a good thing. We too used to enjoy David Frost in the days when his appearances on television were comparatively rare.

My Government will as usual give its full support to any bills that it wishes to pass. Certainly I have no power to stop it. Estimates for the private sector will be laid before you.

Measures will be introduced to make jokes about Princess Margaret, Lord Snowdon and the Duke of Kent's chin punishable by imprisonment in the Tower of London.

Unemployment figures will be reduced by raising the school-leaving age to 32; a government grant will be made available to anyone under the age of 60 who wishes to undertake a further period of study. In England and Wales the age of retirement will be reduced to 55.

My Government will work for the early conclusion of an improved honours system. In future medals and decorations will be sent by recorded delivery post, complete with a tape-recorded message from the Prime Minister, to cut down the number of hours I spend on my feet (at investitures). Further measures will be considered that grant every British subject a title at birth and thereby abolish altogether the need for these tiresome chores.

My Government will continue fully to support the Commonwealth and to encourage investment in developing countries so that Philip and I always have somewhere warm to visit each winter.

25 October 1969   *Buckingham Palace*
Philip still in America. Today, in response to an unscripted question in an interview, he declared that the monarchy would be 'in the red' by 1970. I know Charles' investiture was expensive, but had no idea things were so bad.

We must economize. I shall set an example:

1.   I shall sell off minor pieces of the Crown Jewels. I never wear them anyway.
2.   I shall wear dresses and hats more than once.
3.   I shall try to confine myself to four pairs of gloves a day instead of five to cut down on the laundry bill.
4.   The gin-and-tonics at state banquets will in future be $\frac{7}{8}$ tonic and $\frac{1}{8}$ gin.

Royal Household wages have risen by 126 per cent during my reign. Perhaps these could be cut: I know my staff works for me out of loyalty, not for the money. All the same, must tackle Harold Wilson about a Civil List increase.

26 October 1969   *Buckingham Palace*
During a visit to a nursery school a 4-year-old pressed 2 shillings into my hand and said, 'Here you are, Mrs Queen, I want to help you.' I was so embarrassed. Just wait until Philip comes back from America – he and his big mouth have a lot to answer for.

1970

My first audience with Edward Heath, my new Prime Minister.
I knew that Harold's election timing was wrong. Mr Heath was
quite reserved and is at least from the right party, but I've got
so used to Harold. I miss the lingering smell of pipe tobacco,
the endearing way he always changed into his slippers during
our meetings, the little bits of parliamentary gossip from the
back benches. Life will not be quite the same on Tuesdays
now. I discovered that Heath's passion is organs, so I took him
to see Prince Albert's in the ballroom and he gave a quick
rendition of 'A Life on the Ocean Wave' as we discussed
President Nixon's proposed visit to Chequers.

Received a telegram from Harold: 'Tell Ted not to change
Mary's wallpaper at Number 10. He won't be in office long
enough.'

1971

5 May 1971   *Buckingham Palace*
Teddy came for his weekly audience. He has arranged for the
Civil List income to be more than doubled, from £475,000 to
£980,000 per annum. What a marvellous PM he has turned
out to be. We seem to have recovered from the postal strike
and the engineers' strike and are currently staving off a
threatened miners' strike. Did a walkabout in Coventry, which
is tiring on the feet but was *so* successful in New Zealand last
year. All the newspapers claim that the first walkabout was in
1970, but we actually did one in Malta in 1967 on a wonderful
visit to Sir Maurice Dorman, the Governor General.

Sometimes I wish I could write to the press and tell them

what a load of absolute rubbish they write. My Press Secretary began collecting fabricated stories about us from around the world. Now we cannot get into the Press Office.

15 August 1971   *Royal Yacht* Britannia
Anne's 21st birthday. I wanted to make her Princess Royal as a present, but she said, 'No, Mummy, I want a proper present like everyone else.'

30 September 1971   *Balmoral Castle*
The PM came to Scotland for his obligatory weekend with us. He is the first bachelor to be in Downing Street since Balfour, so I had to pair him off with Mummy at dinner, which did not please her.

'He kept talking to me about cows, Lilibet,' she grumbled.

'Cowes, Mummy, *Cowes*,' I explained.

'A cow's mummy?' she said. 'Now are they heifers or bullocks?'

I don't think Mr Heath really enjoyed his weekend at all. We were celebrating Anne's victory at Burghley, but he doesn't appear to know one end of a horse from another unless you talk in naval terms.

'Anne sat on the stern of the horse, just in front of the poop deck,' teased Philip. Mr Heath failed to appreciate the joke.

'Ah well,' said young Edward later, 'he's very good at funny voices.'

'That's his *own*, dear,' I said.

1972

10 January 1972   *Sandringham House*
Had dinner by candlelight this evening because of the power
cuts. Received a telegram from the Isles of Scilly: 'At least you
had light when I was PM. Harold.'

15 January 1972   *Sandringham House*
We all wore our mink coats to breakfast this morning because
the heating was off and we're trying to conserve coal during
the miners' strike. A new messenger delivered my red boxes
from the station and glanced in through the window. Now
he'll have the lifelong impression that we always dress up for
breakfast.

8 February 1972   *Buckingham Palace*
Mr Heath came for his audience. I am to declare a state of
emergency. I had the housemaids open all the windows for two
hours before he arrived and held a torch throughout our
meeting just to demonstrate that I am not impressed with his
handling of matters. Had a large photograph of Harold Wilson
standing prominently on my desk. Bobo is packing for my
state visit to President Pompidou. At least his rooms are warm
even if the welcome is cold.

24 February 1972   *Buckingham Palace*
Informed my Press Secretary that it seems unlikely we'll be
seeing any trade union leaders at Palace garden parties in
future.

25 February 1972   *Buckingham Palace*
The miners' strike is over.

29 March 1972   *Buckingham Palace*

Opened the Tutankhamun exhibition at the British Museum to mark the 50th anniversary of the tomb's discovery. The queues stretched right round the outside of the building and it took us four hours to get in. I was a little worried about the famous curse, that threatens: 'Death will come to those who disturb the sleep of the pharaohs . . .' Already so many people connected with bringing the exhibits to England have suffered misfortunes. Philip remarked that whatever happens it can be no worse than the curse of the Heath government. 'We disturbed his sleep and look at the misfortunes *that's* caused,' he said.

Andrew teased me over dinner tonight, claiming that my belongings will go on display in two thousand years' time: 'Elizabeth II's mummified handbag, her three strings of pearls, a stuffed corgi, a carefully preserved twinset . . .'

I was not amused. He's obviously inherited his father's appalling sense of humour.

13 May 1972   *Windsor Castle*

A rail strike began. Now we cannot travel on the royal train.

Received a surprise invitation from Pierre Trudeau to attend next year's Commonwealth Conference in Canada. *So* unexpected, as he does not seem averse to a republic. It does, however, give us a good excuse not to accept Mr Kosygin's invitation to Moscow. I might not get out again if I were to visit the Soviet Union, especially as I don't have a passport. I shall send Edward Heath instead.

20 October 1972   *Yugoslavia*

Arrived here for a state visit to a warm welcome but a very small hotel. Bobo was not at all happy with her room so I changed with her. There was no full-length mirror in my room so she and a footman unscrewed one from the wall of the ladies' lavatory and it is now propped up on a pile of books beside my bed.

1973

31 July 1973   *Government House, Ottawa*
In the last month I have travelled 16,000 miles over Canada,
apart from flying back to Britain for a few days to help Anne
with her wedding-present list. Although I have always *been*
Queen of Canada, I now really *feel* as if I am. Everyone seems
to be so royalist and they call me 'Your Majesty' twenty times
in every sentence. There was one hilarious moment when we
were being presented with a picture of a diving bird (known as
a 'loon') by the Mayor, Walter Assef.

   'Your Royal Highnesses,' he began, 'we're so pleased that
you could be here today. Now where's the loon?' Then
everyone danced around the platform trying to locate the
elusive loon. I could not help laughing, and I could see Philip's
shoulders heaving. Fortunately everyone took our outburst in
the right spirit, and it certainly helped our image. As I said to
Philip over dinner this evening, 'I've been Queen for over
twenty years now and I just feel as if I have relaxed into the
role.'

7 November 1973   *Buckingham Palace*
Opened Parliament. Miners, firemen and ambulance drivers
have begun selective strikes, so I glossed over that in the
speech but gave Edward Heath a long hard glare when I came
to the point about my Government doing its utmost to solve
industrial disputes. Philip has gone to Australia to get away
from Anne's wedding preparations. I visited her dressmaker,
Susan Small, today and met the charming Maureen Baker
who is responsible for it. It is beautiful material – and
washable, I was glad to hear.

14 November 1973   *Buckingham Palace*
What a proud mother I felt today as I watched my only
daughter walk down the aisle. A tear came to my eye and then
I remembered that I must not give in to my emotions in front
of 700 million viewers. Not for me the privilege of a quiet

maternal weep. Mark is a sweet boy and has just been voted 'Best Male Head of Hair of 1973' by the National Hairdressers' Federation, which *must* be some kind of joke. Philip and I are giving them a holiday on *Britannia* as a wedding present (it is sailing to Barbados and New Zealand anyway), and Anne can carry out some engagements to forestall any press complaints about the expense.

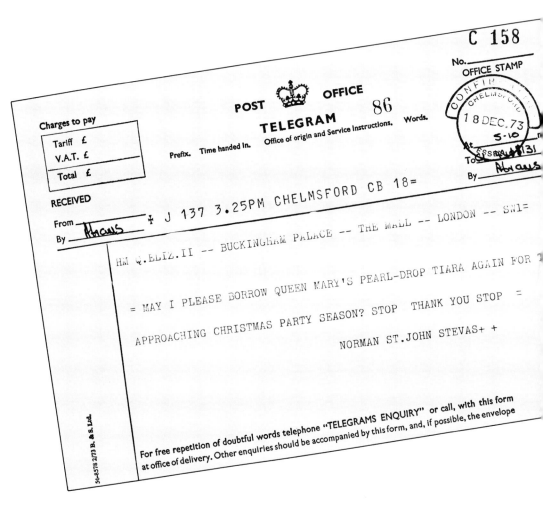

C 158

POST OFFICE TELEGRAM

86 Words.

Office of origin and Service Instructions.

OFFICE STAMP

18 DEC. 73
5·10

Charges to pay

Tariff £
V.A.T. £
Total £

Prefix.   Time handed In.

RECEIVED

From
By

‡ J 137 3.25PM CHELMSFORD CB 18=

HM Q.ELIZ.II -- BUCKINGHAM PALACE -- THE MALL -- LONDON -- SW1=

= MAY I PLEASE BORROW QUEEN MARY'S PEARL-DROP TIARA AGAIN FOR

APPROACHING CHRISTMAS PARTY SEASON? STOP   THANK YOU STOP   =

NORMAN ST.JOHN STEVAS+ +

For free repetition of doubtful words telephone "TELEGRAMS ENQUIRY" or call, with this form at office of delivery. Other enquiries should be accompanied by this form, and, if possible, the envelope

56-8578 2/73 B. & S. Ltd.

12 December 1973   *Buckingham Palace*

The rail drivers' union, ASLEF, has begun a ban on overtime and a three-day week is being introduced to conserve fuel. Mr Heath came to see me this evening.

'And what suggestions do you have, Prime Minister?' I asked, hoping for a solution to the crisis.

'Well, I could play "Oh Come, All Ye Faithful", or would you prefer "We Three Kings of Orient Are"?'

Sent Harold Wilson a Christmas card saying 'Wish you were here . . .'

Bill.

BUCKINGHAM PALACE

Please send a Memo to the Arts Minister to say that although I don't mind him borrowing my tiaras for major theatrical events (at least it saves me having to attend), I do object to him wearing them at fancy-dress parties.

ER

1974

1 March 1974   *Buckingham Palace*

Had to curtail my Australia/New Zealand trip and return to
Britain because of Heath's sudden decision to call a General
Election. From the glorious heat of Australia I arrived back
today to find Britain in the grip of freezing winter, no
electricity, no TV and the Royal Household in line with others
is working a three-day week. I only left the country a few
weeks ago, yet things seem to have got totally out of hand.
The election results were disastrous, with no clear overall
majority, which Heath seems to think is a vote of confidence
in his government. He's taken on the trade union leaders and
lost, and now he wants to join up with the Liberals (with
Jeremy Thorpe as Home Secretary!), which is about as much
use as pouring boiling water into a chocolate teacup. I can't
help feeling that all this compromise is a recipe for disaster.
Coalitions are only appropriate when there's a war on.

2 March 1974   *Windsor Castle*

Sent Princess Alexandra to the travel agents (nobody
recognizes her in public) to get some brochures about cruises
and boating holidays. We sent them off anonymously, in the
hope that Mr Heath will get a longing for the sea again. I
dropped a subtle hint to him today; putting on my caring
voice, I said, 'Don't you *long* for those distant days when you
weren't Prime Minister and could laze around in boats all day?'

   He looked vaguely wistful and shrugged his shoulders.

4 March 1974   *Buckingham Palace*

At 7.12 p.m. Edward Heath resigned!

   At 7.13 p.m. Harold Wilson's car screeched into the
courtyard. He ran into the Palace so fast that I thought he
would swallow his pipe.

   'Never fear, Harold's here!' he chuckled, then added, 'Now
that Mr Day-Lewis is no longer with us, would you not
reconsider Mary for Poet Laureate?'

He tells me that he wants a June election, but I told him to wait until all the strikes have been sorted out first. Quite frankly I don't think my people could cope with another election so soon. Besides, the swingometer gives Mummy a headache. I presented Harold with a new tobacco pouch and he agreed to wait until autumn before going to the polls.

16 June 1974   *Chantilly*
The most exciting day of my entire reign. Highclere romped home ahead of 21 rivals at the Prix de Diana. His father is one of my favourite stallions, Queen's Hussar, and I just knew that he would make it. Everyone shouted, *'Vive la Duchesse!'* and Lord Porchester and I did a little dance in the royal box.

I telegraphed Philip, 'We won, we won!'

'I wasn't aware that we had been at war,' he telegraphed back.

1975

4 February 1975   *Sandringham House*
Edward Heath was defeated by Mrs Margaret Thatcher in the ballot for the leadership of the Conservative Party. Within minutes, I gather, her car was pulling into the Palace courtyard. She told Bill Heseltine that she had 'come to kiss hands with Her Majesty'.

'That's if you become Prime Minister, *not* Leader of the Opposition,' he told her.

24 July 1975   *Buckingham Palace*
I was introduced to Barbara Castle at a garden party this afternoon. She refused to curtsey to me. I was a little taken aback, but showed no reaction. Probably no one has ever curtseyed to her so she didn't know what to do.

'At her age one of her hips might have given way,' remarked

my equerry, grinning. Margaret says she's positive Barbara dyes her hair. Either way, it's the right colour for the Labour party. Noticed some streaks of grey in my *own* hair this evening . . .

25 July 1975   *Buckingham Palace*
Sent for Mr Martyn, my hairdresser. I'll be fifty next year, so I suggested that perhaps we should do something with my hair. He says that he could bleach a piece at each side to make me look older. That's not *quite* what I had in mind.

Margaret and Tony are now living apart. He is in one wing of Kensington Palace, she is in another.

'I'm surprised it's lasted as long as it has,' commented Philip. 'In fact, it amazed me that they left the Abbey together.'

1976

9 March 1976   *Buckingham Palace*
Finally had to make an official announcement that Margo and Tony are to separate and will be getting a divorce. It's a word Mummy has refused to use since 1936, but we can keep it quiet no longer. The press have noticed that M and T arrive at functions in different cars, enter through different doors and insist on eating in different rooms. Things came to a head at least year's BAFTA awards when Tony called my sister a 'trollop' in public. He insisted later that he was talking about 'Anthony Trollope', but Margo was not convinced.

'He knows nothing about literature,' she sneered. 'He thinks "The Pallisers" are people who go to Buck House garden parties.'

I thought this very droll, coming from someone who once asked me if *Forever Amber* was about faulty traffic lights.

KENSINGTON PALACE

1 May 1976

My dear Lilibet,

    Now that I am freed from my duties as a wife, I have decided to occupy my time by setting up a small business of my own. I have undertaken some market research and feel that one up-and-coming idea is computer dating. So I have decided to set up my own agency, called 'DATA-ROYAL' (date-a-royal' - get it?) and will be providing a much-needed matchmaking service for all the eligible members of the European royal house: it will enable Princess Marie-Astrid of Luxembourg, for example, to date Prince Albert of Monaco, Princess Cristina of Spain to get to know Prince Haakon Marcus of Norway, and so on... Isn't it marvellous!
    To join, all they have to do is pay a small dowry and fill in my simple questionnaire:

1. To which titles are you currently heir?

2. How much property, jewellery, etc. are you due to receive on your majority, parents' death, etc.?

3. What is your Civil List (or equivalent) income?

4. How many staff make up your household?

5. Would you prefer your wedding ceremony to take place at St Paul's or at Westminster Abbey?

6. Have there ever been signs of haemophilia in your family?

7. Do you get on well with horses and corgis?

8. From which monarch(s) are you descended?

    When the couple meet for their first date each is advised to wear a recognizable piece of jewellery or medal from his/her country so that they can spot each other instantly. This could be a marvellous way to get Charles married off - and would you like me to sign up Andrew and Edward too while I'm at it?

Love,
Margo

21 April 1976   *Windsor Castle*
Celebrated my 50th birthday. I looked long and hard in the mirror this morning whilst Bobo was brushing my hair and saw Queen Mary looking back.

'Do I really look like my grandmother?' I asked Philip.

'No, Lilibet, dear, of course not.'

That was a relief.

'But there *is* some resemblance to Queen Victoria . . .'

Andrew and Edward sent a card which said: 'Congratulations on your half-century. Only another fifty years and you can send yourself a telegram.'

Charles forgot, but he's very involved in transcendentalism at the moment. I don't discourage him because when he's in a trance we notice the improvement.

2 May 1976   *Windsor Castle*
Harold and Mary came to say their final farewells, although I think he really wanted to know what title I was going to give him. He wanted to be Lord Harold of Huddersfield, but this to me seems to lack dignity.

Lord Wilson of Rievaulx is what we have decided, as it has an aristocratic ring to it. (For all his working-class habits, Harold has a lordly air about him.)

'What kind of damn-fool name do you call that, Ma'am?' he asked, with his customary grace. 'I don't even know where it is, let alone how to pronounce it.'

I asked him why he had decided to resign the leadership so suddenly.

'Leave while you're on top, Your Majesty,' he said, puffing away on his pipe. 'That's my motto. I've sorted out Heath's mess and I've borrowed £1000 million from the IMF: now Jim Callaghan can think of some way to pay it back. Simple!'

18 July 1976   *Buckingham Palace*
Margaret has got very friendly with a 27-year-old gardener called Llewelyn. She must have met him through her dating agency. Had a letter from Auntie Wallis asking how it is that the sister of the Queen can get divorced, yet she as a divorcée

could not marry a king? Got my lady-in-waiting, Mary Morrison, to drop her one of our standard letters: 'Her Majesty thanks you for your good wishes at this time' . . . etc.

20 July 1976   *Windsor Castle*
Purchased a nice little house from Rab Butler for Anne and Mark. It is in Gloucestershire and a real bargain at £425,000. I'm going to mortgage it to them, so they can pay me back over 25 years at £17,000 a year plus interest. It should be a good little investment and it will mean that Philip and I will have somewhere private to stay when we go across for the Badminton Horse Trials. Had an audience with Jim Callaghan (or 'James', as he prefers to be called). Harold got me into the habit of calling him Jim. He's been Chancellor of the Exchequer, Home Secretary and Foreign Secretary, so I suppose there was no other job left open to him.

David Steel has been elected leader of the Liberal Party, so in just over a year I have been faced with new leaders for all three major parties. Now that I've had more experience than all of them put together I really enjoy my weekly audiences, and Mr Callaghan always has a box of dominoes in his pocket in case we ever run out of things to talk about.

25 September 1976   *Balmoral Castle*
A fascinating weekend with the Callaghans. They really are such a charming couple, despite the things Harold says about him. Audrey Callaghan went out of her way to be helpful. At lunch she suddenly began gathering all the dishes.

'Sit down, Audrey,' said Mr Callaghan. 'Her Majesty has staff to do that. You're not at home now.'

I found this very endearing. Over lunch he gave me his life history, from his upbringing in Portsmouth right through to becoming PM. I do admire people who have worked their way up from nothing.

In the afternoon, while Audrey dozed off in Edward VII's favourite chair, Mr Callaghan (or JC, as he likes to be called) and I had a real heart-to-heart. I told him very little. He told me everything.

'I suppose you're disappointed that it's a Labour government in office, Ma'am?' he said.

'To be quite honest,' I answered truthfully, 'it doesn't bother me which party is in government. It makes no difference to my way of life. In my position personality counts for more than political party. But if the PM and I "click" he will be more likely to accept my advice.'

'Very sensible, Ma'am?' he said.

I had another brandy poured for him and had a footman pull my chair up a little closer.

'Now, tell me,' I said confidentially, 'why do you think Harold *really* gave up the premiership?'

'I think he'd done all that he could – he was just going round in circles. And then there was Mary.'

'Mary?' I asked, leaning closer.

'It had deserted her.'

'Oh, it had, had it?' I thought for a moment, then asked, '*What* had deserted her?'

'The Muse.'

'No, it's still there – open to the public once a week, and *we* use it all the time.'

'Not the Royal Mews, Ma'am, the Muse – the inspiring power of poetry.'

'But he resigned so suddenly. When did *you* know he was going to leave?' I asked eagerly.

'Just the week before he left office. It was his 60th birthday and Mary had failed to write a witty poem in his card. That night we were driving along the embankment to cast our vote in the House when he leaned over to me and whispered, "I'm resigning next week, so you'd better get ready."'

'Fascinating.'

'But this must go no further than these tartan walls.'

'It will go no further,' I assured him.

From the Rt. Hon. Sir Harold Wilson, KG.,OBE.,FRS.,MP.

HOUSE OF COMMONS
LONDON SWIA OAA

23rd September 1976

Your Majesty,

I have just received a telephone call from Sir
Harold, who is currently on holiday in the Isles
of Scilly. Mary is apparently composing an ode
for next year's Jubilee, which could (he says)
take until 1978 to complete.

Sir Harold is anxious to know how the Callaghans'
first weekend with you at Balmoral passed. He has
a bet with Michael Foot that it was not as much fun
as when he was Prime Minister. He finds it very
amusing that you've had the hottest weather for 500
years, knowing how the heat plays havoc with the
Callaghan foreign policy. He is convinced that
Jim is planning to put icebergs in the English
Channel to stop any Armada getting across...

I do hope the Duke of Edinburgh's boils have
healed up.

Yours sincerely,

M. Williams

Marcia Williams
Private Secretary

Her Majesty the Queen
Balmoral Castle

1 November 1976   *Buckingham Palace*
Received an official telegram to say that James Earl Carter has
been elected President of the United States. I'm told he is a
peanut farmer from the 'Deep South'. Whatever next! A
cowboy in the White House?

    Mummy telephoned to say the the top Premium Bond prize
has been increased from £75,000 to £100,000. In that case I
shall buy one.

1977

24 January 1977   *Sandringham House*
Received a postcard from Prince Michael in St Moritz, where
he is competing in the world bobsleigh championships.
Delighted to read in the *Daily Express* today from the reliable
Mr Hickey that 'yet another love affair of Prince Michael's has
petered out'. I feel sorry for Michael, of course. After all at 34
it's about time he settled down, but that Marie-Christine
Troubridge, the former Baroness von Reibnitz, was obviously
unsuitable. Not only is she a Roman Catholic, she is *still
married*. Fortunately the girl is sensible. 'Prince Michael still
remains a friend, but my close association with him has
ended,' she says in the newspaper. 'My husband is the most
important man in my life.'

    Why does my cousin always go for married or divorced
ladies? Philip thinks he must be seeking a mother figure.

Mummy and I are helping serve the tea at the Women's
Institute tomorrow afternoon. I do hope that she can
remember how to make it.

22 January 1977   *Sandringham House*
Anne has been prosecuted for speeding. How embarrassing!
On past occasions she's got away with a verbal warning. There
was little that our solicitor, Mr Willis, could say in her defence,

I suppose, as she was travelling at 96 miles an hour, but there was no need for him to plead for 14 days to pay.

'Sorry, Mummy, I thought I was on a horse,' she said, totally unperturbed. This is the first time the child of a reigning monarch has been prosecuted, and it's made worse by the fact that it's *my* court and *my* law. They'll be accusing me of mistreating my children next.

Had a nice 'phone call from Mary Wilson telling me to watch out for Sir Harold and Mike Yarwood doing a double-act on the *Parkinson* chat show. As a prime minister, Harold always did have the timing of a comedian.

1 February 1977   *Buckingham Palace*
Returned to London today after a glorious rest. Now my Jubilee Year begins in earnest. The diary is completely full, as was the PM – of himself – when he came to see me this evening. He's extended fishing limits by 200 miles, which has created more jobs for deep-sea anglers; he's lowered the retirement age for coal miners, creating more jobs down the pits; and last month the strike record was at its lowest for months.

'We've never had it so good,' he beamed. Surely I've heard that somewhere before? It's only the second month of the year and already I'm tired of seeing my face on everything from mugs to chamberpots. When I visited the kitchen they were using Jubilee tea-towels, the chambermaid was dusting my knick-knacks with a Jubilee duster and even Bobo has an apron with my face on it. Have they no respect?

29 May 1977   *Windsor Castle*
Our first free moment in four months, during which I've not had an opportunity to write one diary entry. It all began with a dinner with the Australian High Commissioner at Stoke Lodge, Hyde Park Gate, on 3 February, then before I knew it we were in Samoa, Tonga, Fiji, New Zealand, Australia, Papua-New Guinea, then back to London to present the Maundy money. I launched HMS *Invincible* at Barrow-in-Furness, visited the police in Hendon, had dinner with NATO

foreign ministers at Buckingham Palace, went to the Chelsea Flower Show, Strathclyde, Stirling, Dundee, Edinburgh, and last night slept through a Gala Performance at Covent Garden, and they're only some of the engagements that I can remember. It's like Coronation year all over again, but now I'm 51 and soon to be a grandmother (Anne is expecting), so I feel the strain rather more.

Philip just said, 'Stop moaning. Abdicate if you don't like it.' Always the soul of sympathy, my husband.

Oh, how I'm looking forward to my thanksgiving service, the Commonwealth conference, Trooping the Colour, Stockport, Llandudno, Cardiff, Glamorgan, Portsmouth, Hackney, the North of England, the South of England, Canada, Bahamas, Virgin Islands, Antigua, Barbados . . .

20 June 1977   *The Royal Train*
Philip is queuing in the buffet car, so am taking a moment to relax. Tonight I fulfilled one of my ambitions and met the cast of *Coronation Street*. I hardly recognized Ena Sharples without her hairnet, but she seemed to know who I was. I was so thrilled to meet them all – Alf Roberts, Mike Baldwin, Rita Fairclough, all my favourite characters – in the flesh, and as I've missed every episode for the last year they were able to fill me in on some details. The report I receive weekly from the Lord Chamberlain's Office is hardly quite the same.

21 November 1977   *Royal Box, London Palladium*
Well, I obviously drew the short straw this year, as everyone insisted that it was my turn to attend the Royal Variety Performance. I'm *sure* I was here only last year. I tried to get a concession on the tickets for a block booking, but Lord Delfont insisted that we pay full price.

'Only the Queen Mother, as a senior citizen, gets a discount, my dear,' he said, smiling.

Anyone would think he owned the Palladium. When I arrived the woman presenting me with a bouquet turned out to be his mother, Olga.

CONFIDENTIAL

LORD CHAMBERLAIN'S OFFICE.
ST JAMES'S PALACE, S.W.I.

'CORONATION STREET' UPDATE

Hilda Ogden cleaned the Rovers' Return public house singing what might have been 'Only a Rose' (or possibly 'The Sound of Music').

Hilda argued with Annie Walker, who had accused her of leaving dust in the Snug.

Elsie Tanner accused Betty Turpin of giving her short measures of gin.

Rita Fairclough had a row with Mavis Riley over who should deliver the morning papers. Mavis had a suspected coronary, but was all right again by Wednesday's episode.

Hilda Ogden had a row with her husband Stan, having seen him attempting to give Mavis the kiss of life and misinterpreted the situation.

Gail Potter slipped and hit her head on the deep-freeze in the corner shop. Renee Bradshaw had a stand-up fight with her fiancé Alf Roberts when she caught him giving Gail the kiss of life behind the bacon counter.

Len Fairclough swept Elsie Tanner's chimney with a ferret on a piece of rope and accidentally filled Annie Walker's back parlour with soot. He has been banned from the Rovers' Return. Bet Lynch has been doing Al Jolson impressions behind the bar there.

After being dismissed from the Rovers' Return she was taken on by Renee Bradshaw at the corner shop, who is nursing two black eyes, four cracked ribs and a fractured deep-freeze.

31 December 1977　　　　　　　　*Sandringham House*

Jubilee Year has drawn to a close, and in many ways I'm quite sorry. By the time my Golden Jubilee comes along it will be the year 2002 and I will be 76! I think this must have been my busiest year ever. I've worn out 27 pairs of shoes and have scarcely one pair of white gloves left that haven't been darned. This evening Mummy sat reminiscing about *her* year: she's had a few good wins on the horses, played snooker several times in public and opened a supermarket.

'Have *you* done anything exciting this year, Lilibet?' she asked, jogging the under-butler's hand as he poured her a medicinal whisky.

'About the same as usual, Mummy,' I shouted. She gets a bit forgetful at times and it didn't really seem worth explaining. After midnight, when everyone was doing the hokey-cokey round the stables, Philip and I sat beside the fire in Queen Alexandra's drawing-room and laughed at the experiences we'd had: that awful official photograph, when Bobo put me in a tweed dress and I blended into the carpet; and the telegram from Idi Amin threatening to come to the Jubilee celebrations (we had four rooms knocked into one at Sandringham to accommodate his bed, and then he didn't come). Poor old Sandringham – now 91 rooms are crumbling and will have to be demolished because of it.

Talking of large men, how can I forget meeting the King of Tonga, who is built on the same generous proportions as his mother, Queen Salote? I'm told he weighs 33 stone and has to weigh himself in with the baggage at the airport.

At his banquet I was given my own sucking-pig, a whole turkey, a pineapple and a whole coconut. My plate was a bit full. The King kindly asked me if I would like a couple of lobsters as well.

'Not just at the moment,' I said, smiling. 'Perhaps later . . .' Fortunately I was able to sneak most of it into my handbag when nobody was looking, which was all right until it was searched by an over-zealous policewoman.

'What *are* you doing?' snapped Philip.

'Searching for bombs,' replied the woman.

'But that's the Queen's bag!' he stormed, scratching his head in amazement.

'She's not going to blow *herself* up. Now search everybody else's bloody bag!'

'If she eats the amount of food she's got in there, she will certainly blow herself up,' retorted the policewoman, turning away to frisk the King of Tonga.

I had to smile.

Australia was not so good this year, although the people greeted us with customary affection. 'Down with Liz' and 'Anarchy not Monarchy' said a couple of the banners that almost hit me. I pretended not to notice, but inside I felt a bit flustered, fluffing one of my speeches by saying how nice it was to be in Australia 'in the Silver Jubilee reign of my year', but nobody appeared to notice. Gough Whitlam referred to me as the Queen of Sheba, which I can only assume was a slip of the tongue.

My visit to Scotland got off to a bad start when Scottish Nationalists began claiming that the country should be independent from England. I know that I'm not supposed to make political statements, but I began my speech, 'I number kings and queens of England *and* of Scotland, and princes of Wales, amongst my ancestors. I cannot forget that I was crowned Queen of the United Kingdom of Great Britain and Northern Ireland.' That took the wind out of their sails, and I was quite pleased when the newspapers called it 'fighting talk from the Queen'. That must be one of my better press notices.

In Govan I visited a council house, which the owner was delighted to show me.

'And we have *two* bedrooms here,' she announced proudly.

'It's so useful to have an extra bedroom, isn't it?' I said, just to prove that I really am like them.

Jubilee Day itself was memorable too, and I deliberately asked Bobo to choose an old dress (the one I wore last July to open the Olympic Games in Canada) so that no critic could claim that my celebrations were costing the tax-payer money. The loveliest moment on that day was when Philip gave me a painting, by Linklater, of my favourite horse, Dunfermline, who really has done so well this year, winning the Pretty Polly stakes, the Epsom Oaks and the St Leger.

The only shadow to have fallen on me this year is that my eyesight seems to be failing, and sometimes I have actually read out the wrong speech. In the end I had to succumb and get the royal optician to test my eyes; he confirmed that I needed glasses.

'When your speeches have to be printed in such large letters that you have only six words per page, it is time to do something, Ma'am, before they get too heavy to transport.'

It took a long time to choose some suitable frames, and I even had the Imperial State crown brought from the Tower of London so that I could choose something that would look good while I'm on the throne for the State Opening of Parliament. Each time I found a pair that I liked either Edward told me I looked like Mary Whitehouse, or Philip said I resembled Queen Juliana of the Netherlands (who is years older than me and on the verge of abdication) or else they were just too expensive.

In the end I settled for a pair of National Health frames. I finally plucked up the courage to wear them in Ottawa when I opened the Canadian Parliament on 4 November, thinking that I was far enough from home for it to go unnoticed. I should have known better. Within hours the British press was printing cartoons of me with a white stick and a corgi guide-dog.

ROYAL EYE TEST

H
O N
I S O I
T Q U I M

A L Y P E N S E

1978

2 February 1978   *Sandringham House*

A postcard from Charles, who is skiing in the Swiss resort of Klosters. It seems he is being dogged by the press because he has Lady Sarah Spencer with him and they all assume that he is going to get engaged. To stop the rumour-mongers he has said that he will not marry until he's 30. Why on earth did he not say 40? That would hold them off even longer. There's not the slightest chance he would marry Sarah Spencer, in any case. She's the daughter of Papa's equerry!

4 February 1978   *Sandringham House*

The papers say Charles will marry Princess Marie-Astrid of Luxembourg.

5 February 1978   *Buckingham Palace*

Today Charles has been linked with the Grand Duchess Charlotte of Luxembourg. She's 81, for heaven's sake! Who on earth will they pick for him next – Minnie Mouse?

6 February 1978   *Buckingham Palace*

The Sun suggests that Charles should marry Minnie Mouse . . .

25 February 1978   *Windsor Castle*

Margaret has caused a scandal by taking Roddy Llewelyn on holiday with her to Mustique. I was a little anxious at first but Mummy is sure he has only gone to re-design her garden.

10 March 1978   *Buckingham Palace*

President Tito of Yugoslavia popped in for a state banquet on his way home from talks with President Carter in Washington. The latter kindly sent me a peanut tree to plant in the Palace gardens. Philip likes the idea and thinks we could become self-sufficient in peanuts to use at cocktail parties. President Tito is 85 now but still very spritely, although I was a little disconcerted when he took his teeth out at dinner. Helping himself to half a pound of cherries, he proceeded to spit the pips ten feet across the room into the fireplace. I offered him a plate, which he declined. He is obviously rather proud of his pip-spitting prowess and enjoys displaying it.

Charles' name has been linked with that of Lady Jane Wellesley.

24 May 1978   *Buckingham Palace*
Margaret obtained her divorce today. We watched poor Tony on the 6 o'clock news looking terribly sad.

'I've never seen such good acting,' Margaret sniffed. 'Give him an Oscar, Lilibet.'

She knows very well that I can't award Oscars, otherwise I would have given myself one years ago.

KENSINGTON PALACE

Her Royal Highness The Princess Margaret C.I., G.C.V.O.

and **still** *the Countess of Snowdon*

invites you to a

Divorce Celebration Party

24/25/26/27 May 1978
7.30 for 8.00
R.S.V.P.

Don't bring a friend,
bring a bottle.

31 May 1978   *Buckingham Palace*

Prince Michael brought Mrs Troubridge, the former Baroness Marie-Christine von Reibnitz, to see me this evening. She was a little bit cool – icy, in fact – but perhaps she was just nervous. The Baroness has apparently divorced her husband now and wants to marry Prince Michael. Why does divorce continue to raise its ugly head in my family? Perhaps they do it deliberately so that they can contravene the Royal Marriages Act. Michael needed my consent before he could marry, which placed me in a difficult position. I didn't want to destroy his happiness, but there are so many obstacles. As Supreme Governor of the Church of England, I cannot allow them to marry in my Church, first because of her divorce, secondly because she's a Roman Catholic.

'We could go quietly to a registry office,' he said.

'Sorry, Michael, but as members of the Royal Family we are exempt from the legislation which allows such weddings. You would in theory be living in sin.'

The Baroness gasped and clutched at her pearls.

'But *you're* ze Queen. Change ze law!' she demanded.

'This is England,' I explained, matching her frostiness. 'Nothing is that simple.'

'Zen it's a very silly little country and, by ze way, your curtains do not match ze carpet in zis room.'

I was a bit taken aback, but I later discovered that she is an interior designer.

'You cut your curtains according to your cloth,' I retorted, adapting one of the proverbs I have often used in my speeches to the Privy Council. 'However, Mrs Troubridge, soft furnishings aside, as far as your wedding is concerned, I have decided to consent to it on three conditions.'

Michael looked quite shocked that I could be so hard, but when you have a Labour government you learn to be tough.

'And vot are zose conditions?' she asked, rubbing her finger along the mantelpiece in search of dust.

'One: Prince Michael renounces his rights of succession. Two: any children you have must be Anglicans. Three: you must stop wearing powder blue – it's not your colour.'

I was quite exhausted after the confrontation, but to show that there was no ill feeling I had a copy of the 1772 Royal Marriages Act wrapped and sent to the couple as light reading. I do like to give practical presents.

1 June 1978   *Buckingham Palace*
Received a sweet note and some flowers from Prince Michael, thanking me for consenting to the marriage. He also asked where they could live. The Baroness has a fancy for a grace-and-favour tower at Windsor Castle. I told him that they can have an apartment at Kensington Palace, if she redesigns it. Then we'll have all the divorcées under one roof. The PM called this evening to discuss the General Synod's plans to change the rules about the remarriage of divorced people in the Church of England. I told him that this proposal must be rejected, at least until after 30 June.

30 June 1978   *Windsor Castle*
Prince Michael's wedding day. They married in the Rathaus in Vienna and I sent a representative along, as I had a very important race meeting at Plumpton.

The Baroness is to be known as Princess Michael from now on.

'Surely you could have found an even dafter name for her?' commented Philip, laughing.

'That's quite daft enough, thank you,' I said. 'One must not appear *too* malicious.'

Received an angry telephone call from Margaret: 'You might have warned me that the Kents would be moving into Kensington Palace, Lilibet,' she stormed. 'I've been using that apartment as a wine cellar. Now I suppose I'll have Tyrolean dancing on my ceiling.'

Dear Margo, she does over-react at times.

'Do you think Princess Michael *does* do Tyrolean dancing?' I asked my Private Secretary.

'Not if you tell her it's contravening the Royal Marriages Act,' he replied.

1 November 1978   *Buckingham Palace*

The State Opening of Parliament. I tried to drum up as many members of the family to attend as I could, but they all seemed to have prior engagements. Even Princess Michael was opening a pizza restaurant. I must see that the throne in the House of Lords is resprung. There was an anxious moment when the Lord Chancellor brought my speech – Lord Hailsham really is getting too old for walking downstairs backwards. I almost got up so I could grab him if he fell, but the weight of the crown prevented me.

I noticed Mr Callaghan nodding while I was speaking – presumably in agreement, as if it were all news to him. Strange, considering he had written the speech himself.

1979

22 February 1979   *Middle of the desert, somewhere in Saudi*

Our tour of the Middle East continues. I'm becoming quite adept at eating sheep's eyes, and can drink camel milk almost without wincing. Philip and I had coffee today with His Highness Sheikh Khalifa Bin Hamad Al Thani in Qatar, which was a bit like a Sandringham coffee morning except that I couldn't understand anything that was said to me. We've received lots of very pleasant gifts: a gold, diamond-studded watch, a gold handbag and pinafore of gold chainmail (that will do for Bobo), a gold sword with a mother-of-pearl handle encrusted with diamonds and rubies, and a solid gold camel with palm trees decorated with giant rubies in the shape of coconuts. I gave in return a signed photograph of myself. As I said to Philip, it's the thought that counts.

2 May 1979   *Buckingham Palace*

We are looking forward to our day off tomorrow as it is the General Election, and I'm never allowed out that day in case anything I do or say is misconstrued as political. Mrs Thatcher visited 10 Downing Street today, apparently to measure for curtains and carpets and give Audrey Callaghan a hand with the packing.

3 May 1979   *Buckingham Palace*

Philip and I are sitting in bed watching the election results trickle in. We had a good laugh at the photographs of our trip to Bahrain. There was a lovely picture of me beside a camel looking miserable (I think my feet had swollen in the heat).

'I think you both had the hump that day,' commented Philip, with his usual razor-sharp wit.

4 May 1979   *Buckingham Palace*

Mrs Thatcher, now Prime Minister, came for her first audience today. I felt a little bit intimidated. Philip made sure he didn't have to meet her by hiding in his study.

'No, please, don't stand up,' she said as she came into the room. 'I only want to discuss the legislation on trade union reform, the abolition of the Price Commission, the role of the NEB, the cutting of income tax, and the abolition of legal compulsion on the ILEA to reorganize education on comprehensive lines.'

'Very well,' I said, swallowing hard, 'and congratulations on winning the election.' I noticed that her husband was not with her (most prime ministers bring their entire family for their first audience).

'And where's Denis?' I asked.

'Who?' She placed a pile of papers on my already crowded desk. 'Now, Ma'am, if we could also have a look at the SALT II Treaty that Mr Brezhnev and President Carter are to sign in Vienna next month, in the global context of defensive anti-ballistic missile systems . . .'

She stayed for five hours instead of the expected 55 minutes, which meant that I completely missed an official banquet and a charity gala. I tucked the corgis up in their baskets and Bobo put my hair in a net, but she still didn't take the hint – by then she was talking about Lord Boyd's report on the Rhodesian elections and the effect of Denis Healey's caretaker budget on the financial future of Great Britain. I didn't even get an opportunity to ask if she likes horses. Things are going to be very different.

8 May 1979   *Buckingham Palace*

Mrs Thatcher came for an audience. I had on full evening dress, decorations and tiara so we could pretend that I was due at an important function and could only spare her half an hour. She wanted to know if she could change the day of the Prime Minister's weekly visit from Tuesday to Wednesday. It has *always* been a Tuesday so as not to clash with *Coronation Street*, so I insisted that we stuck to tradition. I did discover that she was Margaret Roberts before she married and that her father ran a corner shop somewhere in the north. I wonder if they are any relation to Alf Roberts in *Coronation Street?* I did mention the Street to her and she asked if it was in one of the council estates that she wished to sell off. I spent the rest of the evening hiding at Clarence House. Mummy always dresses for dinner anyway, so I did not feel out of place.

1980

30 April 1980   *Windsor Castle*

Queen Juliana of the Netherlands has abdicated, at the age of 70. Queen Mary would not have approved! I've made it quite clear to my aides that I don't approve either, which should put paid to any hints that I should give way to Charles.

Princess Michael wants a balcony built at Kensington Palace, probably so that she has something from which to wave to the people.

1 June 1980   *Buckingham Palace*

Charles has bought a house called Highgrove with the profit from his Duchy of Cornwall property and a very good tip that Mummy gave him at Epsom.

Now the press is suggesting he'll be using it as a love nest for himself and Sabrina Guinness.

Mrs Thatcher asked if she could borrow the Crown Jewels for her official Tory Party photograph.

4 August 1980   *Clarence House*

Mummy's 80th birthday, a very special day. As usual she went to her balcony at Clarence House to wave to the crowds. While watching her, Viscount Linley noticed a crack in the upturned flower-pot that she stands on and we just saved her from plummetting over the edge.

'Blast!' said Mummy, kicking the pot with her platform shoe. 'I've stood on that for over forty years.'

'Can you do something about Granny's pot?' I asked Andrew, who promptly returned with Mummy's favourite piece of eighteenth-century Spode.

'Not that!' hissed Margaret. 'It's nearly as old as she is.'

Fortunately Anne found a chamberpot that was exactly the right height so that Mummy could be seen over the balcony. What a practical girl she is. I've offered to make her Princess Royal on her 30th birthday, which is now imminent.

'No, Mummy, it would be bad for my image,' she insisted. 'Now for God's sake shut up about it.'

The papers say that Charles will marry Davina Sheffield.

4 November 1980   *The Ritz*

Margaret's 50th birthday, and we've all been having a jolly time at her party. Mummy has stayed at home as she swallowed a fish bone (we must get her some new glasses), so I seem to be the oldest person here. Fortunately I've brought a couple of despatch boxes with me, so I'm able to sit in a corner and do a little writing. Most of the guests appear to be under 30 and predominantly male. I suppose it keeps Margaret young, having so many youthful friends. She has been doing her Sophie Tucker impression at the piano, which always goes down well, although I couldn't help noting the incongruity of her rendering of 'My Yiddisher Momma'; we may be a mixed bunch, but I can't recall any Jewish ancestors on either side of the family.

Anne announced at the party that I am to be a grandmother again. What a surprise! They both seem so wrapped up in their horses that I didn't think that she and Mark had time for anything else. I expect the baby will have four legs.

According to the newspapers, Charles is to marry Lady Jane Wellesley.

5 November 1980   *Buckingham Palace*
Arrived back home in the early hours to find the first editions of the newspapers announcing that Anne is pregnant. We can trust nobody. I wonder if it was that spotty waitress serving the caviar who split on us? Her eyes were much too close together for my liking.

Had an early breakfast with my press office, during which we decided to release the news of Anne's baby officially before most people have had an opportunity to buy a newspaper. That will wipe the word 'exclusive' off their headlines!

The newspapers have today decided that Charles will marry Angelika Lagansky . . .

9 December 1980   *Buckingham Palace*
'Hurricane Maggie', as Philip calls her, swept in this evening for the usual audience. She wanted to discuss her summit meeting in Dublin with Charles Haughey. Philip jokingly said to her, 'Perhaps you can sew up the hem on my study curtains and make the Christmas pudding while you're here.' He always jokes about how much Mrs Thatcher manages to fit into one day on a large scotch and four hours' sleep. She made quite a good job of the curtains and managed to ice a Christmas cake before she left.

Ordered 500 Christmas puddings from Fortnum & Mason as presents for the staff.

Lord knows when I'm going to fit in all my Christmas shopping.

10 December 1980   *Buckingham Palace*
Harrods came today and set up a display in the White
Drawing Room so that I could shop for presents.
Unfortunately most of the items were too expensive. With 783
people on my present list my £50 budget does not go very far.

Received a Christmas card from the new American
president, Ronald Reagan, and his wife Nancy.

'Wasn't he in that film with the monkey?' asked Charles this
evening. 'Fancy having an actor as President!'

'We've just had a peanut farmer in the White House, so why
not?' quipped Philip.

Ex-President Carter has suggested that his daughter Amy
would be a suitable bride for Prince Charles. He's obviously
desperate to retain some kind of position in society.

1981

1 January 1981   *Sandringham House*
Charles has brought a girlfriend to Sandringham for the first
time for the New Year house party, Lady Diana Spencer –
quite a sweet girl, very attractive but very shy and really much
too tall for Charles. In fact she's almost as tall as Princess
Michael.

I had a quiet lunch with Diana today to see whether she
might, even so, be suitable for Charles. Certainly she uses the
right cutlery (we had seven courses – quite a test). I had
deliberately had fish knives placed on the table to see if she
would use them (we weren't having fish). She did not, so she
obviously knows her etiquette. I regaled her with the story of
my disastrous visit to Morocco last autumn when King
Hussain treated me like someone visiting an unemployment
benefit office. He kept me waiting two hours in the heat and
dust with no explanation, and when he *did* arrive he was
discourteous. Being a monarch does not give you the right to
treat everyone as if they are beneath you.

'The secret is to make people feel important, even if they aren't,' I told her. Diana listened intently, appearing to be interested even though she must have been rather bored, so she obviously possesses the basic qualities required for royal duty. As she left the room I could not help noticing that she was wearing earphones. Poor girl – I simply had no idea that she was deaf.

2 January 1981   *Sandringham House*
Charles and Diana came to see me today to ask if they could get married.

'Have you ever been divorced?' I asked her.

'No,' she replied, looking at me from under her fringe in wonderment.

'Good. In that case I consent.'

I am very relieved that Charles is at last paired off. After all, I was married with two children and had been sovereign for seven years by the time I was his age.

'About time that boy pulled his finger out!' exclaimed Philip. Coming from him, that was an expression of rapturous approval.

17 January 1981   *Sandringham House*
Listened to Margo on the radio today: she was a guest of Roy Plomley on *Desert Island Discs*. Of all his guests she must have been the most experienced as she spends half her life on an island in the sun. I think she agreed do it on mainly in order not to be outdone by her ex-husband – Tony has already been on. He said that his favourite piece of music was the Waltz from Act One of Tchaikovsky's *Swan Lake*; Margaret said hers was the Waltz from Act Two. Typical! He also chose 'Land of My Fathers', because of his Welsh origins, so she quite deliberately selected 'Scotland the Brave'. She also had 'Rule Britannia', as that's one of my favourite pieces.

She wanted to take a well-stocked drinks cabinet as her luxury item, but Mr Plomley pointed out that this could give a bad impression. She insisted that she'd only chosen this so that she'd have a good supply of empty bottles to send messages in, but in the end she was persuaded to settle for a piano instead.

Journalist Jean Rook has written that I should pluck my eyebrows. How dare she! It would make all my portraits and our entire coinage look wrong, not to mention putting Jeannette Charles out of a job.

24 February 1981   *Buckingham Palace*
We officially announced that Charles and Diana are to marry, and now all hell has been let loose. The Palace is under siege from reporters, photographers and film crews. Diana looked most unsure of herself, which is not surprising seeing that her father embarrassed us all by appearing *outside* the Palace railings with his wife Raine and taking photographs.

Charles and Diana have filmed an interview with Alastair Burnet (I shall probably have to knight him in the Birthday Honours now), which seems to be *de rigueur* now for royal couples. I hid myself behind a screen throughout the interview to ensure that they didn't make such a ridiculous mess of it as Anne and Mark did. Every time one of them began to make a silly remark, I coughed. The royal physician was summoned by my Private Secretary in case I had croup. Margaret and Mummy were among the first people here to toast the happy couple, both bringing their own supplies of champagne, which was very thoughtful of them.

5 May 1981   *Buckingham Palace*
Mrs Thatcher's weekly elocution lessons really are making a difference – the pitch of her voice is now considerably lower. I remember I managed to make my own voice lower by listening to Edward Heath.

Mrs Thatcher is aiming to sound authoritative yet caring, which should stand her in good stead with Ronald Reagan.

Margaret insists that the easiest method of altering one's voice is to gargle with gin and smoke 60 cigarettes a day. It's certainly worked for her.

BUCKINGHAM PALACE

10th June 1981

Lady Diana Spencer
c/o HM Queen Elizabeth the Queen Mother
Clarence House
London SW1

My dear Diana,

As your future mother-in-law, and indeed the incumbent of a position to which you will yourself one day succeed, I should like to take the opportunity to pass on some advice which, as your wedding day approaches and you begin to undertake royal engagements, you may find helpful.

1. Learn how to stand. We, and by that I mean all members of the royal family, invariably have to stand for long periods. This can cause varicose veins and play havoc with one's feet. Never stand with your feet together; instead, position them at least twelve inches apart and distribute your weight evenly. It may not be elegant — nobody expects elegance of royalty anyway - but it's comfortable.

2. Cultivate the art of small talk. You need a list of stock phrases at the ready, especially for a walkabout. My favourites are:

   'How many hours have you been waiting?'
   'How long have you worked here?'
   'Do you live here?'
   'I'm the Queen. Perhaps you recognize me from the postage stamps.'

   If you do not know what to say, simply murmur 'How interesting!' and walk away, or say, 'Isn't the Queen Mother marvellous for her age!'

3. Do not use the phrase 'My husband and I' when you are married. That is _my_ catchphrase. I suppose you could say, instead, 'Charles and myself'.

4. Practise a glum expression in the mirror for serious occasions — what my Press Secretary, Michael Shea, calls a 'Miss Piggy' face (a strange expression, however — I can't recall Pinky _or_ Perky ever looking serious). It helps to have three facial expressions: (i) happy; (ii) serious; (iii) animated.

5. Don't let your father in front of the television cameras again, if you ever want to be taken seriously.

   Finally, my dear, God bless and welcome to the Firm!

   Elizabeth R.

13 June 1981   *Buckingham Palace*

Trooped the Colour. I knew that the thirteenth is an unlucky day, but I did not realize *how* unlucky until this morning when a young man fired a gun at me. Burmese reared a little and I had to cling on for dear life, because if I'd fallen off in the Mall I would be forced in future to wear a hard hat whilst riding, and they ruin one's hair. When I heard the shots I was uncertain what the noise was at first – whether it was the Crown Equerry's pacemaker exploding again, or whether the high-fibre diet that Charles is on had had some unsavoury repercussions. Fortunately the boy only fired blanks and no lasting harm was done, so I carried on as normal. As I stood on the balcony later in the day for the fly-past, Mrs Thatcher burst through the Balcony Room and practically pulled me aside.

'She's obviously trying to take my place now,' I fumed to myself, but she was really only concerned for my welfare and insisted that I either wear a bullet-proof cape in future or give up Trooping the Colour altogether.

'Why not let Princess Michael stand in for you?' she asked.

I maintained a dignified silence.

29 July 1981   *Buckingham Palace*

Now two of my children are married: only two to go. First Anne was carried off by Mark, and today Charles by the Spencers. It's like having one's family taken over by a chain store. But it *was* a beautiful wedding. We used St Paul's Cathedral because Westminster Abbey was too small to accommodate all of Charles' so-called ex-girlfriends, Andrew's current girlfriends, camera crews and journalists from around the world, and the few friends and family that could be squeezed in. Diana's dress was made of satin and lace with pearls, bows and everything but the kitchen sink sewn on to it – but very splendid as she floated down the aisle like a barrage balloon. Charles, in full dress-uniform, looked very handsome, too and when Diana fluffed her lines (calling him 'Philip' instead of 'Charles') he quite deliberately fluffed his so that she did not feel too bad about it.

There was a slightly embarrassing moment when Philip invited Raine Spencer into his carriage, instead of Diana's mother, Frances Shand-Kydd. Thank goodness the incident didn't become a fight. I pretended not to notice and carried on talking to Lady Fermoy, one of Mummy's ladies-in-waiting and Diana's grandmother. I think Raine Spencer was slightly upset because her mother, Barbara Cartland, was not invited – but we did not want anyone upstaging Mummy in the chiffon-and-feathers department.

We had a lovely party this evening, which reminded me so much of my own wedding day, especially as everyone kept remarking that it was the wedding of a future queen.

The party was given at Claridges by Patrick Lichfield's sister, Lady Elizabeth Shakerly, who had done a marvellous job with the decorations. The foyer was adorned with silver birch sprayed blue, and the ballroom had real green apples hanging from brightly coloured maypoles holding up a vast canopy. Unfortunately we had made the mistake of inviting Margo's ex-husband, Lord Snowdon. I rather miss having Tony come to photograph me so it seemed an excellent opportunity to see him again.

However, it wasn't long before an ugly scene developed on the dance floor when M and T collided during a military two-step.

'Still trying to crowd me, are you?' hissed Margo, then carried on dancing.

Thereafter she was in one of her moods, demanding lobster when there were only fishcakes on the menu – at which point I discreetly retreated to the powder room before I was called upon to arbitrate.

I had great fun dancing with King Olav of Norway, who does a very good tango, but was rather embarrassed when I spotted the King of Tonga in the crowd and went over to greet him. It was not until we got on to the subject of the Commonwealth that I discovered that this large gentleman was a saxophonist from New York. Strange – he bore a strong resemblance to Queen Salote. Maybe I'd had too many dry martinis. Ah well, never mind – Tongan or not, the saxophonist too turned out to be a wonderful dancer.

David Frost (I can't imagine what he was doing there) also kept asking me to join him on the dance floor, but I told him that my card was full and perhaps I would be free at the next royal wedding.

Philip was extremely merry. He spent much of the evening doing the foxtrot with Nancy Reagan, who I'm sure appreciated having the company of a younger man. We did not leave until 1.30 a.m. – way past my usual bedtime. By that time Philip was wearing a vulgar hat with 'Kiss Me Quick' on one side and a picture of Charles and Diana on the other, which I had to forcibly remove from him before he walked outside, otherwise the waiting press would have had a field day.

Bobo was busy packing for our Commonwealth tour when we got home.

'Bobo, what are you *doing?*' I exclaimed. 'It's the middle of the night – and our Commonwealth tour was 29 years ago!' Poor dear, she's over 80 now and perhaps getting a fraction too old for the job.

30 July 1981   *Buckingham Palace*
It's business as usual after the five-month furore leading up to the wedding. Held an investiture this morning and got through 160 people in less than an hour, which must be my record. Nearly everyone wanted to discuss the wedding, so I just said, 'Yes, wasn't it lovely?' to each of them, smiled, then turned to the next. It does so help if they all discuss the same topic.

Knighted Harry Secombe, as he is one of Charles' favourite Goons.

'They call me Sir Cumference now, Ma'am,' he giggled, patting his tummy.

'You should have been a comedian, Mr Secombe,' I replied.

'CHARLES AND DIANA TO DIVORCE,' announced one of the tabloids today. I suppose it was inevitable (the headline, not the divorce).

Mrs Thatcher borrowed three Canalettos, a Renoir, six Hepplewhite chairs and a table made from an oak tree that had once stood on the battlefield of Waterloo. She says she wants to make Number 10 appear 'fitting for a prime minister'. I think the television people must be due to film there, as she also asked to borrow a pair of pearl earrings from me.

 Royal Mint

7 Grosvenor Gardens, London, SW1W OBH. Telex 267321 Telephone 01 828 8724-8

21 September 1981

Her Majesty Queen Elizabeth II,
Balmoral Castle,
Nr. Ballater,
Aberdeenshire,
Scotland.

Your Majesty,

    Whilst we at the Royal Mint were watching the wedding of the Prince and Princess of Wales on television recently, we became aware that your Majesty has matured somewhat since the current coinage bearing your portrait was minted.

    It has been pointed out to me that Your Majesty's 55th birthday was celebrated this year, which seems to present a suitable anniversary to update the portrait in line with the passing years.

    I have taken the liberty of enclosing a few design sketches for proposed new coins and would be grateful if you would give them your gracious consideration during the remainder of your holiday in Scotland.

    I await Your Majesty's comments.

Your obedient servant,

H. Potts

H. Potts

Damned cheek!
Tell him we'll stick with
the coins we have at present.
I like them. EIIR

P.S. Have I really 'matured somewhat'?
— makes me sound like a piece of stilton.

BALMORAL CASTLE

H. Potts Esq.,
Royal Mint,
7 Grosvenor Gardens,
London SW1W OBH

24 September 1981

Dear Mr. Potts,

I am commanded by Her Majesty the Queen to thank you for your letter of 21 September 1981.

While Her Majesty sympathizes with your wish to change the coins of the Realm, she feels that her likeness is symbolic rather than literal and therefore requires no updating.

Yours sincerely,

Sir William Heseltine K.C.V.O., C.B.
Deputy Private Secretary

BALMORAL CASTLE

25 September 1981

Cyclax Limited,
17/18 Old Bond Street,
London W1X 4AY

Dear Sirs

Please send the following items to Buckingham Palace in time for Her Majesty's return at the end of the month:

24 x 600 ml bottles of All Day Face Firmer
12 x 100 ml bottles of Anti-Wrinkle Cream
12 x 100 ml bottles of Extra-deep Cleansing Milk
10 packets of Pearl Face Powder
15 Milk & Honey Face Packs

Yours faithfully,

Mary Morrison

Lady-in-waiting to HM the Queen

---

8 December 1981   *Buckingham Palace*

Summoned all the Fleet Street editors to the Palace today as the reporters are making Diana's life a misery. Those of us who were born royal obviously find it easier to cope with press harassment than someone like her who has known personal freedom and anonymity. Pregnancy has made her liable to burst into tears at the drop of a hat, which can be awkward, especially if she's in the throes of naming an aircraft carrier.

The reporters have also noticed her wine-gum addiction – eight packets a day, now, so it's obvious she's deeply unhappy. I tried to get her on a horse to cheer her up, but that failed. I even bought her a corgi as a child substitute until the baby arrives. What else can a mother-in-law do? Every move she makes is reported in the press, and she's not the only one who's getting tired of it. I'm lucky to get half a column nowadays.

I must do something sensational to get more coverage. Even when I wear one of my really awful hats I'm ignored, and if my skirt blows up in the wind no one bothers to take a photograph. I deliberately wore trainers under my gown at the State Opening of Parliament, but not a single person noticed. Even Jean Rook has stopped criticizing my headscarves.

For the press briefing, Michael Shea had called all the editors to the 1844 Room to discuss an 'unspecified problem'. Not one of them knew that I was listening next door. Andrew had rigged up a special contraption so that I could hear the conversation. Mr Shea observed that Diana is a victim of her own popularity, and maybe the press should try hounding those members of the family who actually seem to enjoy it. Once the editors had been given a lecture they were all brought in to meet me, which for many was a shock – especially those who have criticized me in the past.

'Why should she not be photographed?' asked a Mr Askew, editor of the *News of the World*. 'If she goes into a shop she is in public.'

'All she wants to do is buy wine gums,' I insisted.

'If she wants to buy wine gums could she not send a servant to get them?'

'That is an extremely pompous remark, if I may say so,' I stated firmly.

How dare he use the word 'servants'! People that we employ are our staff.

Michael Shea quickly changed the subject.

'I hear that Mr Brezhnev is on monkey glands to keep himself young,' he stuttered.

'Well, they don't seem to be doing him much good,' I said.

20 December 1981   *Windsor Castle*
Christmas approaches again. This year we are going to revive the old tradition of a festive show in the Waterloo Chamber, just like the pantomimes we did when I was young. This time it's a tableau, similar to those Queen Victoria used to have.

The Windsor Christmas Spectacular
Waterloo Chamber, 25 December 1981

CAST
(not in order of succession)

Widow Twankey	..HRH the Princess Margaret
The Good Fairy	HM Queen Elizabeth II
The Bad Fairy	HRH Princess Michael of Kent
Baron Hardup	HRH the Duke of Kent
Little Red Riding Hood	..HRH the Princess of Wales
The Ugly Sisters	HRH the Prince Andrew
	The Hon. Angus Ogilvy
Grumpygrew the Goblin	HRH the Duke of Edinburgh
Prince Charming	HRH Princess Alexandra
Pantomine Horse	HRH the Princess Anne (front end)
	Captain Mark Phillips (rear end)
Abanazer	HRH the Prince of Wales
Princess Charming	HRH the Duchess of Kent
The Broker's Men	HRH Prince Michael of Kent
	HRH The Duke of Gloucester

Dance troupe: Zara Phillips, Peter Phillips, Lord Frederick Windsor, Marina Ogilvy, James Ogilvy, Earl of St Andrews, Lady Sarah Armstrong-Jones

Director, impresario and tea-boy	..HRH the Prince Edward
Choreography	..HRH the Princess of Wales
Costumes	Mrs 'Bobo' Macdonald
Scenery construction	..Viscount Linley
Music	..Pipe Major McTavish
Refreshments	HM Queen Elizabeth the Queen Mother
	assisted by HRH Princess Alice, HRH Duchess of Gloucester

1982

President Reagan and his wife Nancy are here on a state visit.
They have hinted for a long time that they would welcome
any invitation I might extend to them, so in the end we had to
ask them over, especially as they were with the Pope on the
5th, the President of France on the 6th and the Prime Minister
of Italy on the 7th. They landed this evening on the Windsor
golf course in a helicopter. We did not allow members of the
public into the Castle precincts as cheering and flag-waving on
this occasion would look as if we had sunk to the American
way of doing things. Instead I had a small band of Grenadier
Guards, who played Beethoven's Ninth as the Reagans
arrived. Mr Reagan put his hand on his heart and stood to
attention, thinking it was the National Anthem, until Nancy
kicked him. I introduced them to members of the family and
to Mrs Thatcher, who curtseyed deeply then flung her arms
around Mr Reagan, kissing him firmly on the cheek.

'And this is a painting of one of my ancestors,' I said quickly,
taking the President by the arm and pulling him from the
embrace. I know the PM is very concerned with our relations
with America, but at times she goes too far.

Tonight I gave a State Banquet for them. Proposing a toast,
President Reagan said, 'Here's looking at you, kid!'

I thought he said, 'Here's looking at Euclid,' and told him
that I knew very little about Greek mathematicians.

8 June 1982   Windsor Castle
I rose early this morning and invited the President to come
riding with me.

'I might as well,' he said. 'I can't sleep with those damned
bagpipes blaring outside the window.'

'That's Her Majesty's alarm clock, Ronnie,' hissed Nancy.

'Gee, can't we send her a clock radio like the one we've got?'

After breakfast we rode out from the Mews. I was on
Burmese and I'd given the President Centennial, an 8-year-old

gelding who had once appeared in a cowboy film in Canada. More than 100 photographers surrounded the Castle to take pictures and to my astonishment Mr Reagan began answering questions. I galloped on ahead before a journalist spoke to me. I was livid with the President and gave him a very frosty glare. Later he apologized to me.

'Burmese wasn't used to stopping at that point, so I had to move on quickly,' I replied.

Philip took Nancy Reagan to the Royal Mausoleum to see where my ancestors are buried. She had 57 security men with her. Philip had the usual local policeman from Datchet. It was quite a relief when the Reagans eventually left today as I was getting a little tired of being searched for explosives every time I stood close to the President. I'm relieved that our security is less obvious.

9 July 1982   *Buckingham Palace*
I was woken soon after 7 o'clock this morning by the sound of breaking glass near my window. I'd been having a marvellous dream in which I had just won the Derby by 21 lengths, and at first I thought the sound of glass was Lord Porchester trying to open a bottle of champagne. I opened my eyes and looked at the clock beside my bed. It was 7.17 a.m.

'Typical!' I thought. 'My new housemaid has got the time wrong.'

Ever since Bobo retired to Windsor I've had a succession of incompetent assistants who bring me morning tea at all hours of the day and night. Then I noticed a figure attempting to pull the curtains from the middle.

'Pull the cord at the side, the cord!' I shouted. Suddenly daylight flooded into the room and I saw a man in jeans standing by my windows. Was this Philip in disguise again, re-enacting the Milk Tray commercial? I reached for my glasses and had a closer look.

'Sorry, Your Majesty, Ma'am,' said the man and sat down on the foot of my bed. He was definitely not Philip – far too polite. I reached for the panic button and pressed hard.

'Get out!' I roared, and pointed to the door.

'Have you got a cigarette I could have?'

'I don't smoke,' I explained, 'and if you're here for today's garden party you're too early.'

'I've found an ashtray, but I need a cigarette,' he explained, holding up a piece of jagged glass and dripping blood on to my bedspread. I wasn't too bothered because I've wanted a new bedspread for a long time and this provided me with the perfect excuse for getting one.

'I think there might be a cigarette under the bed,' I said, and as he disappeared beneath my queen-sized posture-sprung I pressed the panic button again with my foot and dialled security with my hand.

'Can you see one?'

'No.'

'Well, go further under,' I commanded, then I ran to the door and looked out into the corridor. There was no one – no footman, no policeman. Then to my relief a housemaid came round the corner carrying a tray.

'Quick! There's a man under my bed!' I hissed.

'Cor, one of them erotic dreams, was it, Ma'am?' she giggled.

'No! There really is a man under my bed.'

I pushed her into the room and under the bed to have a look.

'Quickly!' I shouted to a footman returning with the corgis from their early-morning constitutional. 'There's a man and a housemaid under my bed.'

'I *bet* it's that Muriel, Ma'am. She's a caution with the men.'

The whole episode was like a nightmare.

'It's coming to something when a queen is not safe in her own bed,' I said at breakfast.

'Oooh! – you're telling me, Ma'am!' exclaimed an under-butler. 'If you knew what went on in the footmen's quarters after lights out . . .'

I got Viscount Linley to screw some security locks on my bedroom door.

17 July 1982   *St Mary's Hospital*
In hospital for the first time in my life, to have a wisdom tooth
removed. I think if I ever have to come again I shall go
privately.

19 July 1982   *Buckingham Palace*
My long-serving bodyguard is being blackmailed by a
prostitute and now has to leave. The doctor has prescribed
valium for me.
   ' "QUEEN FOUND WITH MAN IN HER ROOM, HAS
TEETH OUT AND SAYS FAREWELL TO GAY
DETECTIVE" – I think I'll sell that headline to *The Sun*,'
joked Philip, sympathetic as ever, over dinner. Drank an extra
glass of Phylosan. Tried to speak to Charles on the telephone
but was told that he is on the sea bed with 'Mary Rose'. My
world is falling apart.

20 July 1982   *Buckingham Palace*
Passed the afternoon watching the racing on television with
Mummy, visited Hampton Court Stud after that and spent the
evening playing with my new personal computer (a gift from
President Reagan). I've logged all my horses into the computer
and can now plan their breeding programme at the touch of a
button. Even before a horse is born I can plan the number of
foals it will have. Demonstrated the machine to Mrs Thatcher.
   'I have one, Ma'am,' she said. 'I use it from time to time for
re-shuffling the Cabinet.' She had really only come to gloat
about her Falklands victory, I think, and now considers herself
a latterday Churchill.
   'I'm not sure that's how you're meant to do the V-sign,
Philip,' I said as he raised two fingers to the PM.

26 September 1982   *Balmoral Castle*
The final day of the Thatchers' weekend with us, and it has
been quite an exhausting time. Mrs Thatcher, who enjoys
walking, took us on a 30-mile hike after lunch. Diana
immediately flew back to London, claiming a possible
pregnancy. Mummy, Denis Thatcher and Margaret seemed to

be getting on too well to separate, so Philip, Charles and I accompanied the PM through the hills. Marching through the heather she regaled us with stories of the Falklands campaign; she said she had heard that Andrew made a number of direct hits and was one of the best scorers. Before dinner this evening she gave a hand in the kitchen, and I notice that she has completely rearranged the furniture in the Blue Drawing Room. Having changed for dinner she found time to redesign the table decorations before joining us for a pre-prandial drink. Before retiring to bed we sang, 'There'll Always Be an England,' and 'Keep the Home Fires Burning', at her instigation.

27 September 1982   *Balmoral Castle*
The Thatchers left for London today and the place seems strangely empty without them. They were due to leave after breakfast but did not actually depart until after lunch as their son Mark was driving to fetch them and apparently lost his way somewhere near Cardiff. I'm sure I spotted Carol Thatcher lurking outside in the heather at one point, probably trying to get an exclusive story for Fleet Street. After they had left I discovered that during the night the PM had re-wallpapered her bedroom and whitewashed the ceiling; she has kindly left me a little light reading – 56 state papers to sign.

1983

3 March 1983   *Washington, DC*

Our state visit to America has been dogged by bad weather. Tempests, tornadoes and floods have hit us wherever we have been and I have spent the entire tour wearing a plastic mackintosh and a headscarf. At one point on the Reagans' ranch I found myself wrapped up like a Michelin Man against the elements whilst Nancy wore a gold lurex cocktail dress and, strangely, not a hair on her head was ruffled by the wind and rain. It is the worst weather we have ever known – so bad that we've had to abandon most of the itinerary. I don't mind missing the speeches, the endless parades of drum majorettes or the motorcades, but it is a shame not to see the sights when one has come so far.

4 March 1983   *HMY Britannia*

Trouble is brewing at the Palace. We have been sent a copy of *The Sun* with the headlines 'QUEEN KOO'S ROMPS AT THE PALACE' above an article claiming that Andrew has taken an actress home with him while we've been away. This amazing exclusive was reported by my ex-storeman Kieran Kenny. After long consultation it has been decided to take out an injunction to prevent any more such stories. As we are out of the country it will all have blown over by the time we return home. By a late post we received a postcard from Andrew asking my permission to escort a Miss Katherine Stark out to dinner.

   'You see,' I said proudly to my press secretary, 'Andrew even asks my permission to take a girl out to dinner, and he's never even heard of this "Koo".' The newspapers always get hold of the wrong end of the stick.

30 March 1983   *Buckingham Palace*

We were welcomed home by the Foreign Secretary at the Palace. It's strange that I have to be welcomed into my own home, but such are the peculiar traditions of my country and we wouldn't have them any other way. Mrs Thatcher came this evening to show me the new £1 coin that will replace the old £1 note next month. It's quite nice, but as I don't ever handle money it will not change my life.

1 May 1983   *Buckingham Palace*
Mrs Thatcher has invited us to spend a whole day with her at Chequers, on any date between 11 and 15 May. Unfortunately I have a very full diary, I told her, so we cannot possibly go.

ROYAL WINDSOR HORSE SHOW

HOME PARK, WINDSOR

11th, 12th, 13th, 14th, 15th MAY, 1983

Complimentary Admission Ticket
TO ONE SESSION ONLY

TO BE GIVEN UP AT ENTRANCE TO SHOWGROUND

NOT TRANSFERABLE

---

10 June 1983   *Buckingham Palace*
Mrs Thatcher won yesterday's General Election with a majority of 144, so it looks as if she is here to stay.

'Why don't you offer her a bed here on audience nights?' suggested Philip. 'She stays so long.'

'Why would she want a bed?' I asked. 'She never sleeps.'

At least I am spared having Michael Foot turn up every Tuesday. I'm told that his best suit once belonged to Clement Attlee.

30 June 1983   *Windsor Castle*
Andrew is taking out a model called Katie Rabbett. 'It's pronounced "Rabbay",' he tells us, but Philip will insist on calling her 'Rabbit'.

'Num, num, num, what's up, Doc?' he shouted across the quadrangle this evening in a Bugs Bunny voice as Andrew was about to go out on a date.

2 October 1983   *Balmoral Castle*
Received a telegram from Downing Street to say that Neil Kinnock has been elected Leader of the Labour Party, replacing Michael Foot.

'Don't worry, *he'll* never be Prime Minister,' declared a note from Mrs Thatcher, 'By the time I'm out of office he will be of pensionable age.'

That did not stop Ronald Reagan becoming President of the United States, I warned my Private Secretary, Bill.

'Don't worry, Ma'am,' said Bill. 'He couldn't be PM. The dresses and high heels wouldn't fit him.'

25 December 1983   *Windsor Castle*
Any hope of a peaceful Christmas was destroyed on Christmas Eve when Charles and Diana arrived with Prince William. He's only $1\frac{1}{2}$ but into everything, and very destructive. One of my favourite brooches (one of Granny's chips and part of the Cullinan diamond set) was flushed down the lavatory, along with one of the corgis. Both were thankfully retrieved. We missed most of my speech today because William played with the television knobs and although the man from DER was very prompt in turning up to mend it the circus was on by the time he'd finished.

'Obviously a good judge of speeches,' commented Mummy, but I was not pleased. It had taken three days to film that speech and now I've missed it. I quickly sent a footman to fetch a copy of the script so I could give a live rendition at teatime, despite the youngsters shouting, 'Rubbish! Get off!' and 'Bring back Esther Rantzen!'

This evening we played charades, but the Duchess of

Dinner Honoring
Her Royal Highness The Princess Margaret
Countess of Snowdon

Maine Lobster en Gelée
Fines Herbes Sauce
Melba Toast Parmesan

Suprême of Chicken à l'Orange
Wild Rice with Almonds & Raisins
Artichoke Hearts St. Germain

Belgian Endive & Watercress Salad
with Goat Cheese

Sorbet en Surprise
Petits Fours

Hanzell Vineyards Chardonnay 1978
Schramsberg Crémant Demi-Sec 1979

The White House
Saturday, October 1, 1983

P.T.O.

Dear Lilibet,

Top Table 10.50 p.m.

Having such a fun time in Washington! Mr Reagan keeps calling me Maggie and means to think I'm Mrs Thatcher half the time. I've been wearing my tiara since breakfast so that he knows I'm royal, but each time he sees me he tells me how much he enjoyed meeting Princess David. (suppose 'Diana' does look like 'David' when you can't read.) I'm plodding through the endive + goat cheese, longing for a smoke. Thanks, sis, for sending me here! Yawn. Yours. Love Margo.

Gloucester, dear Birgitte, almost ruptured herself doing 'Itsy-bitsy-teeny-weeny-yellow-polka-dot Bikini'. (I think that one turned out to be a Dustin Hoffman film.) We immediately sent for an osteopath, who says that she should be ready to resume her engagements in April.

1984

1 January 1984   *Sandringham House*

It snowed. I wish I could be like Margaret and stay in bed all day. We had a fire drill this morning just for something to do. This evening Philip and I played *Scrabble*, but he got very cross when I managed to get the word 'queen' with my 'Q' on a triple letter and stormed off to bed early. We were able to watch a video of his last World Wildlife tour, which gave us a good giggle, especially when Charles ran the film through backwards. Margaret laughed so much that she nearly set fire to the sofa.

2 January 1984   *Sandringham House*

It snowed again. This evening we put on an impromptu concert to amuse ourselves. Mummy did her rendition of 'There's a One-Eyed Yellow Idol to the North of Khatmandu,' which always has us spellbound and is apparently so like that of the late Bransby Williams. Margaret sang 'Only a Glass of Champagne', while Princess Michael complained about the cold. Edward read an extract from *Troilus and Cressida*, playing Deiphobus, Margarelon and Thersites, which I enjoyed, but it did not go down as well as the music-hall acts. I was then persuaded to have a go at singing 'The Boy I Love Is Up in the Gallery' to Philip – great fun. Who would have thought he was still capable of blushing?

   Afterwards we took it in turns to think of puns for newspaper headlines. Andrew's 'Where there's a Will there's a Di-saster' was considered one of the best, given the chaos my grandson had been causing that day with Diana's cassette collection. She says her Duran Durans will never be the same again.

She played the piano for us later, which was very enjoyable but her repertoire is *very* limited. She can only play one thing – eight bars from the first movement of Rachmaninoff's Second Piano Concerto.

'That's it, Di. Always leave them wanting more!' shouted Philip as she ran from the room in embarrassment. I only hope that she will have learnt a few more bars of it by next year.

12 March 1984   *Buckingham Palace*
The miners went on strike today. Mrs Thatcher came for an emergency meeting.

'Don't worry, Ma'am,' she said. 'It will be over in a day or so.'

I do hope she is right as we have mostly coal fires. We can't afford to run the central heating here.

Had a dress fitting today and was persuaded to wear shoulder pads for the first time in decades. I felt like an American footballer, but shall slip them in for any engagement that Diana is attending.

2 April 1984   *Windsor Castle*
Brünnhilde has sold her latest holiday snaps to a Sunday newspaper. We spend our lives trying to avoid having our private photographs publicly printed, and she *sells* hers for publication! I know that the Kents receive nothing from the Civil List, but there are limits to what one should do for money.

Margaret and Tony appear to be friends again, which is good. He is to take some official photographs of her for her visit to Bermuda this year. I know that she appreciates warm countries so I try to make sure that her engagement diary covers only the warm parts of the globe. I think she has now opened every shop and public house on Mustique.

22 June 1984   *Buckingham Palace*

Margaret fulfilled a lifelong (well, long-held, anyway) ambition to become an actress by appearing in the BBC radio serial *The Archers*. She was playing herself – rather well, I thought. Philip says she's been playing at being Princess Margaret for years.

BUCKINGHAM PALACE

SUGGESTED GUEST LIST FOR INFORMAL LUNCHEON PARTY

The Archbishop of Canterbury – *to say Grace (and perhaps tell some of his Vatican jokes)*

Oliver Reed – *to mix the drinks*

John Inman – *for his gaiety*

Samantha Fox – *for intellectual conversation*

Shirley Williams – *for fashion tips*

Delia Smith – *to help out with the cooking*

William Whitelaw – *for his Margaret Rutherford impressions*

Michael Aspel – *Charles can talk to him about toupées*

Nigel Dempster – *we'll give him the quote of the year – which he won't be able to use without being in breach of confidence!*

Sir Kenneth Newman – *to see that nobody steals the silver*

Princess Alexandra – *she enjoys a free lunch and doesn't get out much, poor dear*

Mark Phillips – *to make up the numbers (that's why Anne married him, after all)*

15 September 1984   *Buckingham Palace*

I have become a grandmother once again – Diana gave birth to another son this afternoon. This time Diana and I had a long chat so that the mistakes that were made when William was born could be avoided.

'Don't leave hospital looking like a dishevelled shopgirl,' I told her. 'We are royal and must be seen to be dignified at all times.'

Even when I went to hospital to have my wisdom tooth out, my hairdresser set to work the moment I came round from the anaesthetic.

Next I told Charles to make sure that they had chosen a name for the baby.

'It can only be a boy or a girl and you've had plenty of time to choose names,' I said, 'so let's release a name as soon as the baby is born.' It stops days of pointless speculation in the press, and, which is more important, it stops Mummy running a book on what the name will be. When William was born she made a killing at 100-to-1 as the only person in Clarence House to pick the correct names.

16 September 1984   *Buckingham Palace*

Diana is learning fast. She left hospital today looking immaculate in red, with her hair beautifully set, *and* the baby's name, 'Harry', was released immediately. I was delighted with her performance. So was Charles, by all accounts – but then he was more closely involved than I.

22 September 1984   *Balmoral Castle*

The Thatchers' weekend in Scotland has come round again. Nowadays we are fully prepared. I wore an ankle bandage – that put paid to any really long walks – and Margaret and Mummy stayed at Birkhall. When they arrived for dinner, Mummy kept her off-the-face hat clamped firmly to her head throughout the meal and, I was later to learn (to my absolute horror), she had a pocketful of fish bones at the ready just in case she felt like making a hasty retreat.

I showed Mrs Thatcher lots of baby photos of Prince Harry,

whereupon she quickly produced pictures of her twins when they were infants.

'I had my son and daughter at the same time. I was studying to become a barrister then, so I couldn't really spare much time for childbirth.' What impeccable organization!

She then produced a quiz that she had devised during 'Question Time' in the House of Commons. This comprised anagrams of politicians' names such as 'I Hires Smalwilly' for Shirley Williams, 'Ee, Shady Neil' for Denis Healey, 'We Had Dearth' for Edward Heath, and so on. She has also become rather adept at telling jokes.

Neil Kinnock was conducting a group of his constituents around the Houses of Parliament when he found himself confronted, in the House of Lords, by the Lord Chancellor, Viscount Hailsham, in full regalia. The Chancellor, recognizing him, called out, 'Neil!', and with that all the constituents fell to their knees.

Philip and I in turn told her about one of our Ghillies' Balls at Balmoral (Andrew made a rude remark at this point which I did not quite catch). At the ball we really let our hair down and dance with all the staff on the estate. One year King Badouin and Queen Fabiola were here staying with us, and Queen Fabiola found herself dancing with the estate carpenter.

'And what do *you* do here?' she asked him. When he told her she had no idea what a carpenter was, but knowing that she should make polite conversation she said, 'Oh, my husband would have been a carpenter – had he not been the King.'

Mrs Thatcher did not laugh. She never seems to get anybody else's jokes.

1985

28 February 1985   *Buckingham Palace*

Visited *The Times*, now celebrating its 200th anniversary. I spoke to one of the correspondents about the miners' strike, which is almost one year old.

'It's all about one person really,' I said, carefully avoiding Mrs Thatcher's name so as not to cause controversy. By the time the evening papers came out, the headlines were screaming, 'QUEEN BLAMES SCARGILL FOR MINERS' DISPUTE.'

I was hardly back at the Palace before Mrs Thatcher was on the telephone congratulating me for making a public statement.

3 March 1985   *Buckingham Palace*

The miners' strike has been called off after all this time. Who says that I reign but do not rule? I must speak out more often in future.

Bought myself a new Daimler Sovereign to celebrate – a snip at £26,000. I've had my old number plates switched to the new car so that Philip won't notice. Must now economize. Am asking the Ministry of Defence to cut the number of military bandsmen by 560. Nobody will notice a few less bugles at Trooping the Colour, and this should save a bit on the £36 million the Ministry spends every year on music.

22 March 1985   *Windsor Castle*

Anne appeared on Terry Wogan's television show this evening, which should boost the BBC's ratings (she is *so* popular at the moment). Any time now I may persuade her to become the Princess Royal. She obviously has a great future as a chat-show host and has a much more acceptable accent than Mr Wogan. I was so proud of her. She is one of the few members of my family who never embarrasses me in public. I wonder if I could arrange for her to have her own series, or perhaps she could commentate at the *Horse of the Year Show.*

She'd like that. Perhaps I'll arrange an informal luncheon for the relevant people . . .

11 April 1985   *Buckingham Palace*
The Canadian Prime Minister, Brian Mulroney, visited me for an audience today complete with television crew. Sensing an election campaign ploy I told him quite firmly that a filmed audience would not be possible. Had I allowed *him* to be filmed then Mrs Thatcher would have been here with Sir Robin Day and a camera crew before you could say 'general election'.

15 April 1985   *Buckingham Palace*
Mrs Thatcher came for her audience. Before she arrived her private secretary rang and asked what I was wearing as the Prime Minister did not want to clash.

'Tell him I never notice what she's wearing, so it doesn't matter,' I said.

While she was with me, explaining Mr Gorbachev's announcement about the Soviet freeze in deployment of nuclear missiles in Europe for six months, the late news on television revealed that Princess Michael of Kent's father, Baron Gunther von Reibnitz, had served as an officer in the SS. Within seconds every telephone in Buckingham Palace seemed to be ringing.

'This is the worst scandal this century, Ma'am,' said Mrs Thatcher. 'It could undermine the entire royal family and shake its very foundations.'

'Thank you, Prime Minister, for your words of comfort,' I said, glaring at her. 'Whatever her past, she is member of the royal family now and we shall all pull together.'

16 April 1985   *Buckingham Palace*
The Press Office had no problems getting the Princess on to TV-AM for an exclusive interview. She did rather well, I thought – at least she appeared human. I felt almost sorry for her. It is now established that her father was 'de-Nazified', just like Claus, Queen Beatrix of the Netherlands' husband. Had a quiet lunch with Princess Michael and promised her my

support. She is to take a prominent part in the state banquet for President Banda of Malawi tomorrow, and I've invited her to join me at the Badminton Horse Trials on 8 May. This always seems to work. Not so very long ago I quickly got rid of the myth that Anne and Diana had fallen out by making them appear in public together at every available opportunity.

29 April 1985   *Windsor Castle*
No sooner has the Princess Michael problem blown over than a scandal erupts involving Charles. I had to step in very promptly to prevent his celebrating Holy Communion with the Pope today. One day he will be King and head of the Church of England. Had he attended a Catholic Mass he would have betrayed his birthright. After all, Prince Michael had to renounce his rights of succession to marry a Roman Catholic – I'd have had *him* down on me like a ton of corgis if Charles had taken part in a Catholic ceremony.

'Sorry, Mother, I just didn't want to offend the Pope,' he spluttered down the telephone. Sometimes he's too well-meaning for his own good. What with the Bishop of Durham doubting the Resurrection and my Archbishop of Canterbury becoming a puppet on *Spitting Image*, I sometimes despair of the Church.

'Visit the Buddhists, the Mormons or the Moonies, but not the Catholics, Charles,' I said. 'It's more trouble than it's worth.'

15 June 1985   *Buckingham Palace*
Trooped the Colour. Nobody noticed the missing 560 bandsmen, thank goodness.

18 June 1985   *Windsor Castle*
My favourite week of the year – Royal Ascot. Am determined not to stake such high bets this year. As I never carry money I always have to borrow the stake from someone, and it's so easy to get carried away.

Mrs Thatcher and her husband joined us today. While I was trying to watch the races the PM insisted on telling me about the Social Services Secretary's announcement that pensions and unemployment benefit are to rise by seven per cent in November, but child benefits blah blah blah . . . two million householders blah blah . . . smaller rate rebates . . .

'Very interesting, Prime Minister,' I said, peering through my binoculars at the course.

'A government motion approving the Green Paper proposals on the reform of social security was carried by 335 to 196 votes,' she continued. I quite saw the reason for Denis Thatcher's jumbo-sized hip-flask.

'Is she always so enthusiastic about her work?' I whispered.

'Always,' he replied. 'She'd like to file me under "D", but I don't fit into the cabinet.'

'Where's the Prime Minister gone?' I asked Philip, noticing that she had disappeared.

'She saw that you were deep in conversation, so she's gone to creosote the fence at the back of the Royal Enclosure,' he replied.

3 September 1985   *Balmoral Castle*
Anne has been doing a live phone-in on Radio 4. I was going to ring in with a question, just so that she would hear a friendly voice, but the lines were engaged.

Told Lady Crabtree to begin packing for my forthcoming tour of ten Caribbean countries in 26 days, the climax of which is the Commonwealth Conference in the Bahamas.

'But you don't leave until the ninth of October,' she insisted. 'I'll pack the night before.'

She is so much quicker than Bobo.

9 October 1985   *Belize*
Arrived here with one suitcase and a hold-all. Normally I would have had 37 trunks, but then Bobo always did pack too much.

'Two days in each country,' said Lady C briskly. 'You only need a couple of outfits and a tiara.'

It certainly cuts down on puzzling over what to wear each day, I must say. Philip's valet has packed 52 suits for him and it is taking him much longer to dress.

BUCKINGHAM PALACE

CHRISTMAS PRESENT LIST 1985

Philip	— carriage driving socks
Mummy	— elastic support hose
Charles	— polo socks
Diana	— black tights with bows at back
Anne	— waterproof socks
Mark	— thick socks
Andrew	— navy socks
A's current girlfriend	— Biggles-motif legwarmers
Edward	— pink socks
Margaret	— fishnet tights
Viscount Linley	— white socks
Sarah Armstrong-Jones	— popsocks
William	— combat socks
Harry	— fluffy socks
Alexandra	— stockings
Angus	— tartan socks
Prince Michael	— sports socks
Princess Michael	— economy pack of tights
Richard of Gloucester	— socks
Birgitte of Gloucester	— tights
Eddie of Kent	— socks
Katie of Kent	— tights
Bobo	— elastic bandage
Gloucester children	— socks
Kent children	— socks

1986

An embarrassing incident occurred today. We often encounter
hostilities in Australia and New Zealand, but as everyone
there originates from convicts one has come to expect it.
Today, however, someone scored a direct hit with an egg,
which means that my coat will have to be dry-cleaned.
Somehow I became the victim of a Maori demonstration. I've
had breasts bared at me (Philip pretended not to notice, but I
saw him take more than a second glance) and been squirted
with water, which blew back on the squirters and over the
waiting press men. That was quite amusing – and one can only
hope that a few British gossip columnists were among them.
Finally – the eggs.

'It would have been worse if they'd hit you on the head,
Lilibet,' said Philip comfortingly, 'and worse still if they had
been hard-boiled.'

At a banquet tonight I joked that I preferred my New
Zealand eggs for breakfast, but I have purchased half a dozen
and now have them at the ready in my handbag. At the
slightest sign of trouble in future I shall throw them back.

1 March 1986   *Sydney, Australia*
It is so pleasant to visit Sydney again and see the opera house
that I opened on a flying weekend here. There are very few
places in the world that I have not visited now, and so it's
good to see something familiar on each tour. As the only
countries I have not been to are China and Russia, I've asked
my private secretary to arrange a trip to China later this year.
Deng Xiaoping, the Chairman of the Communist Party, is 80
this year, so it seems a fitting time to go.

Once again my clothes are being criticized by the Australian
fashion writers. When will they realize that I am a
grandmother and not the Princess of Wales. 'HAS THE
QUEEN ONLY GOT ONE PAIR OF SHOES?' shrieked one
newspaper. No, I have six, but only one pair is really

comfortable. What's more they match my black patent-leather handbag. If I were to wear new shoes every day I would be crippled.

'That's you, Lilibet – comfort before style,' said Philip, although I'm not sure that I appreciated the comment.

Had vegemite and wallaby pie followed by kiwi-fruit pavlova at a dinner this evening. I long to get back home to rack of lamb and fresh strawberries. There's absolutely no place like Windsor . . . or Sandringham . . . or Balmoral.

10 March 1986   HMY Britannia
Received a communiqué from Mrs Thatcher saying that she has signed a treaty with President Mitterand to allow the Channel Tunnel to go ahead: 'Sorry that you were not consulted, but you were wandering around the antipodes at the time.'

How dare she! I'm not sure that I want to become a mere appendage of Europe. There will be ructions when I get home.

19 March 1986   *Buckingham Palace*
Prince Andrew came to see me today, hand in hand with that ginger-haired girl that he was seen skiing with at Klosters this year – quite pleasant, and the daughter of Charles' polo manager, I believe. Ronald Ferguson is a decent chap, too, although his eyebrows are a little too bushy for my liking. It seems that Andrew wants to marry Sarah, and I could see little objection, apart from the fact that she nudges me in the ribs each time she tells a joke. I wait until I think she's reached the punchline, then I smile and change the subject. I'm sure that the fake dog thingy that I found in the corgis' basket was something to do with her, but I can't be certain. It could have been Edward's idea of a joke. Unfortunately Mrs Thatcher, arriving here for her weekly audience, noticed it.

'That would *never* happen in Downing Street,' she said smugly. I asked about our Civil List increase, which quickly wiped the smile off her face.

I'm hoping that the wedding can be arranged for some time between Ascot week and Balmoral, when there's a bit of a lull in events. A wedding is always good for morale, and maybe it will put an end to Andrew's playboy image.

Spent the evening helping Mummy ice my 60th birthday cake. One disadvantage of being Queen is that it's impossible to keep your age a secret.

THE KENNEL CLUB
1-4 Clarges St., London W1Y 8AB

Telephone: 01-493 2001

24 March 1986

Your Majesty,

Thank you for registering your latest dozen corgi bitches. We note that they will be available for servicing in the summer of next year.

Thank you so much.

We remain, Ma'am, your humble servants,

M. Harry

21 April 1986   *Windsor Castle*

My 60th birthday! How time flies. It seems like only yesterday that Margaret and I were just ordinary little girls growing up here at Windsor.

I've seen my grandfather and father on the throne and twelve prime ministers at Downing Street, I've travelled further than any other monarch, I'm in the *Guinness Book of Records* for shaking more hands in one day than anybody else, and I should have a medal for endurance considering the number of Royal Variety Performances and galas that I've sat through in 34 years as Queen.

This morning we attended a service in St George's Chapel, Windsor; then I quickly drove to London, where children presented 50,000 daffodils to me in the Palace forecourt, followed by a show at Covent Garden. In the early evening I felt rather silly walking around Covent Garden market in evening dress and tiara on a scheduled walkabout, but everyone I met seemed to be enjoying themselves. We then rushed back to Windsor for a party, while I checked on the guest rooms and food preparations (the King and Queen of Spain are due here tomorrow on a state visit).

Received a lovely card from Bobo – addressed to Queen Victoria, but still, the thought was there.

24 April 1986   *Windsor Castle*

Received word that the Duchess of Windsor has died peacefully at her home in the Bois de Boulogne. I telephoned Mummy at Clarence House, but her Private Secretary, Major Griffin, told me she was at Epsom. Obviously she had not heard the news.

23 July 1986   *Buckingham Palace*

Andrew and Sarah's wedding day. As a present I gave them the titles of Duke and Duchess of York. Recognizing how silly 'Princess Michael' sounds, I didn't want Sarah to be saddled with 'Princess Andrew'. She is certainly a fun-loving girl and in many ways ideal for Andrew, although at times I wonder about her suitability to be a member of the royal family. She lumbered down the aisle today like a Land Army girl, waving to all her friends, and stuck her thumb in the air when she saw me. As the archbishop was saying, 'Do you take this man . . .?' she mouthed to me, 'I jolly well do, what!' I was so relieved that the television cameras were not on her at the time.

It was not until after I had consented to the marriage that I discovered that Sarah's parents are divorced. Both my sons have married the products of broken homes: I do hope that it will not be catching. After all, their own family is perfectly normal.

26 July 1986   *Buckingham Palace*
I had to get Bill Heseltine, my private secretary, to write to *The Times* today, following its story last week that there is a rift between the Prime Minister and myself – an allegation that my press secretary, Michael Shea, is supposed to have leaked. Mrs Thatcher may have an abrasive and uncompromising style, not listen to anything I say and seldom take my advice, but I would never criticize her to anyone . . . other than Michael Shea, that is.

29 July 1986   *Buckingham Palace*
Charles and Diana's fifth wedding anniversary. I gave them a weekend in Paris as a gift. His is in August, hers in September.

On my physician's advice I visited a heart specialist today.

'With all respect, you are 60, Ma'am,' he said. 'It would be wise to go for a routine check.'

I had no engagements this morning, so thought it would be fun to go. I had every possible type of test and was relieved to hear that my heart is fighting fit. Just before I left the doctor gave me four tips for healthy living:

1.   *When you are working make time to go off for ten minutes on your own, just to have a break.*

        Is he serious? My schedule is always timed down to the last second and I am *never* alone. Even when I go to the lavatory a Woman of the Bedchamber stands guard outside the door.

2.   *Never take work home.*
      I literally live over the shop at Buckingham Palace. How can I *not* take my work home? The PM calls in at all hours of the day and night, and even if Philip and I have one evening a week to ourselves watching the television, I find that I crop up after the epilogue to be reminded yet again of my role.
3.   *Listen to other people – don't always be the leader.*
      But I am the Queen. If I don't lead, who does?
4.   *Always let your feelings out – talk to anyone who will listen.*
      That's the one thing I cannot do. Apart from my immediate family, I have to be on my guard with everyone at all times.

  I think I passed the medical but failed the advice.

30 July 1986   *Buckingham Palace*
It had to happen. A journalist spotted me arriving at the heart specialist's. Now the world thinks I'm on my last legs. One of Charles' aides was seen checking his diary to find a suitable Coronation date in 1988. I hate to disappoint them all, but I am determined to send myself a telegram in the year 2026.

30 August 1986   *Buckingham Palace*
Andrew and Sarah are back from their honeymoon and I must get down to some serious work. I tried to get in touch with Madame Vacani, who taught me to dance when I was a child, but sadly she died years ago. However, her daughter Betty agreed to help me out by teaching Sarah how to walk less like a stable-girl and more like a duchess. It will not be easy, but it must be done. Next we have to sort her wardrobe out. No matter how much Sarah spends on clothes, she never quite brings it off, while Diana always looks marvellous. One journalist said yesterday that Sarah reminded him of 'a pig in the parlour curtains', which is not what I expect of one of my daughters-in-law.

21 September 1986   *Balmoral Castle*
The summer in Balmoral has just not been the same this year.
Young William and Harry have created so much havoc that
half the household has resigned. Sarah and Andrew think it is
a huge joke when one of them pushes someone into the
strawberry patch or in the swimming-pool; the Duchess of
Gloucester had a lot of trouble getting the mud stains out of
her skirt, and Mrs Thatcher did not take too kindly to her
ducking either: there are some things that no amount of
hairspray can withstand.

The press has been making a fuss about Princess Michael's
début as an author – the latest of her ploys to earn the Kents
some money. It's all very well, but she has reproduced huge
chunks of other authors' books, which really is not cricket.

1 October 1986   *Balmoral Castle*
Edward is to join the Royal Marines, which I'm a little worried
about because he's such a sensitive boy. It's Philip's fault: just
because he's Captain General of the Marines he thinks that
every young man should be toughened up. I've packed the
woolly bedsocks that Mummy knitted for him and a hot-water
bottle, plus a very large tube of Germoline; these should see
him through it all.

2 October 1986   *Buckingham Palace*
We are being attacked in the press. The stories of the last week
include 'Fergie in Tears After Bust-up Over Koo' and a
malicious non-story ('I Snorted Coke in the Palace Loo') which
Margaret swears is not true. We seem to be the innocent
victims of a circulation war. Received a postcard from Edward
asking for his teddy bear.

12 October 1986   *Peking, People's Republic of China*
My first visit to China. It's quite an experience – everyone is so
small. I had to review the troops in Tien-an-men Square when
I arrived and I felt as if I were in Lilliput.

'Lilibet in Lilliput,' laughed Philip, but President Li Xiannian
did not get the joke. He is a nice man with a very throaty

voice. He asked after Princess Margaret and invited the Prince and Princess of Wales to China, so he's obviously not averse to a bit of commercialism. He also spoke of Winston Churchill through his interpreter. I assume he's never heard of Margaret Thatcher.

'Thank you for coming to see an old man like me,' said Deng Xiaoping when I met him, which was rather endearing. He is renowned throughout the world for spitting and smoking, but he did not spit once during our meeting.

Tonight we were given a banquet which included sea slug. For me this was the Chinese equivalent of sheep's eyes, but I don't think anyone saw me secreting the foul substance in my handbag. Everyone was amazed at how adept I was at eating with chopsticks – the weeks of practice at Balmoral have really paid off. We were served only ten courses tonight. I gather that ever since I entertained the Chinese General Secretary, Hu Yaobang, at Buckingham Palace with our traditional three courses, they have been cutting down in China.

13 October 1986   *Peking, People's Republic of China*
There were major scuffles today as thousands of pressmen tried to photograph me. We were in the 'Hall of Complete Harmony' at the time the fighting broke out.

Philip and I fulfilled an ambition – walking along the Great Wall of China. I walked further than planned up the steep slopes just to dismiss reports that my heart is in a bad way. Sir Geoffrey Howe and Bill Heseltine, on the other hand, were visibly out of breath and mopping their brows.

14 October 1986   *Shanghai, People's Republic of China*
Philip has confessed to a Scottish student that he found Peking 'deathly boring' and 'ghastly' and that if we stayed here much longer we would all end up with 'slitty eyes' – a classic case of dentopedology. He insists that his remarks were meant jokingly, but I doubt the Chinese will share his sense of humour. I *still* don't, and I've lived with it for years. I can just

see the headlines in Britain tomorrow: *The Sun* will proclaim, 'Philip gets it Wong' and the *Star* will call him 'The Great Wally of China'. When will he ever learn?

Ah well, at least he seems to have got the message: he refused to be photographed with a banana later on today.

24 October 1986   *Buckingham Palace*

After our visit to China and Hong Kong it's been bliss to relax in my new kimono with my feet up. Philip ate his breakfast with chopsticks today – he claims to be really 'into' the oriental 'scene', as he calls it – but I did insist on using a knife myself for spreading the marmalade. I also refused to join him in a sea slug for lunch.

I was just catching up with some back issues of *Horse and Hound* when my lady-in-waiting brought me a magazine that contained an 'exclusive interview' with Princess Michael of Kent.

'What's Brünnhilde up to now?' asked Philip suspiciously.

'It's all right, she's promoting her book,' I said. 'She can't embarrass us this time.'

How wrong can you be!

'I'm fed up with kissing babies and cutting ribbons. I tell you it bores me rigid,' was one of her choice quotes.

'Look at this!' I exclaimed to Philip. 'Princess Pushy says she hates doing charity work and she's "more royal than any of us"!'

'I don't know how she works that one out,' he grumbled. 'All the countries in which she has relatives are republics.'

'And she says that the Duchess of York is common – "all that ghastly winking",' I continued, hardly able to believe my eyes.

'Hmmmm. She says that, does she?'

Philip looked thoughtful: 'She does talk *some* sense then.'

I shall have a stiff word with her and tell her to stay out of the public eye for at least six months. Otherwise I shall ban her permanently from standing on the Buckingham Palace balcony with us.

25 October 1986   *Windsor Castle*

Summoned Brünnhilde here to see me. I was late getting back from a visit to the Hampton Court Stud and had kept her waiting. She was in a foul temper when I arrived.

'I've been here over an hour,' she snapped. 'Time is money to me, you know.'

'I'm terribly sorry,' I said. 'What am I keeping you from? Are you selling a story to the *News of the World*, or do you have a transport café to open?'

That took the wind out of her sails.

'I have to earn my living,' she insisted. 'I don't get a penny from ze Civil List, you know.'

'No, dear, you wouldn't. The Civil List is for members of the royal family,' I replied.

I then presented her with a list of future engagements for her to undertake: judging baby shows and opening hospital maternity wings – all very harmless.

'Now, what about this allegation of plagiarism?' I asked her.

If looks could kill, Charles would now be king.

'If you copy from only *one* source it's plagiarism,' she announced. 'I took notes from *several* sources: zat's called research.'

Commando Training Centre
Lympstone
Devon

1 December 1986

Dear Mum,

I've been in the Royal Marines for 82 days, 3 hours and 27 seconds now and I can't stand it any longer. When I agreed to come here as an acting second Lieutenant, I thought it would be a theatrical job.

I didn't mind it when we were in the jungle war against drug traffickers in Belize, as that was quite exciting. I could pretend I was John Mills in one of those old war films - and I can cope with the 30-mile yomps over Dartmoor, swimming through icy lakes and being hurled through water-filled tunnels with backpack and rifle; I am enduring the gruelling obstacle courses and the constant bullying - but Mum, they actually expect me to make my own bed, polish my own boots and do my own laundry! It's just not on. And I loathe my green beret. Berets just don't suit me.

Please, please, please, please, Mum, you must do something to get me out of here. I know that Dad will do his nut, being Captain General and everything, but if I have to wash another pair of muddy underpants I shall go mad.

Love,

Edward

x x x

153

1O DOWNING STREET
LONDON SW1A 2AA

8th December 1986

Your Majesty,

As I promised at our weekly audience, here is my list
of proposals for the next New Year's Honours. There
seem to be so few people who haven't already received
an award. We may have to use the telephone directory
for your Birthday Honours.

I look forward to your comments, as usual.

Margaret.

KNIGHTHOODS

Andrew Lloyd Webber *Should I have heard of him?*

Terry Wogan *Oh yes, Anne was very good on his show*

The cast of Yes, Prime Minister *Not again*

Spike Milligan *Another goon? How many more?!*

DAMES

Margaret Hilda Thatcher *Isn't this a little premature, Margaret?*

Barbara Windsor *No - people might assume she's a relative*

Jean Alexander *Yes, yes! Hilda Ogden's a national treasure*

Danny La Rue *Is this the one who does Edna Everage?*

The Most Honourable Order of the (Bath) ← *about time too!*

C.B.E.

Ken Livingstone (for all the hard work he is
doing for the Conservative Party) *I can't argue with that.*

Des O'Connor *Only if he agrees to retire*

O.B.E.

Jeannette Charles ⎫
Mike Yarwood   ⎬ *looks a bit like nepotism ....?*
Janet Brown   ⎭

Nigel Havers *Yes, he's so dishy*

M.B.E.

Wayne Sleep *Yes, that will keep Diana happy*

Simon Rattle *Yes, "   "   " Charles "*

Anthony Andrews *Yes, "   "   " Anne "*

Samantha Fox *No, that would make Philip too happy*

Jonathan Ross *??? Someone who can't even
pronounce his own name?*

*What - no news-readers
this year?*

155

1987

2 January 1987   *Sandringham House*
Edward has resigned from the Royal Marines because he found
the uniform too itchy and everyone laughed at his ideas for
staging their Christmas pantomime. Philip is furious with him
and they had an enormous row over lunch today, which I
tried very hard to ignore by feeding the corgis with roast
potatoes. What poor Eddie will do now I just do not know.
Maybe I should have let him join the Royal Ballet School
when he first suggested it. After all, he's always looked good in
tights.

4 January 1987   *Sandringham House*
I have decided that at 61 I am too old to ride side-saddle at
Trooping the Colour, so got the Palace press office to
announce that I am going to retire Burmese and it's not worth
training another horse. If I say I don't want to do it any more
the papers will say *I'm* getting too old, but if I use Burmese as
the excuse no one will be any the wiser.
    Anne has whisked Edward off to Gatcombe Park as Philip
has threatened to shoot him.

8 January 1987   *Sandringham House*
Sarah is very boisterous and reminds me very much of
Margaret when she was young, although my sister had far
more control over her facial expressions. It's not good for a
duchess always to have her mouth open and her eyes out on
stalks. I think Andrew encourages her antics, and together
they go a little bit too far. They went out for a walk with
Charles this morning, both wearing very large rubber ears.
    Anne telephoned, threatening to shoot Philip unless he
leaves Edward alone. She always did enjoy a hunt.

18 January 1987   *Sandringham House*
The water pipes burst over Margaret's bed during the night.
She was absolutely furious and thought it was one of Sarah's

pranks, but I told her I very much doubted that it was this time.

'Poor old Princess Margaret. She's always getting into hot water,' squealed Sarah, thumping me in the small of my back. I was quite winded and couldn't speak for ten minutes.

A telegram from the Prime Minister announced that inflation is down, interest rates are down, she has arranged a summit with Mr Gorbachev and she'd be happy to pop over and sort the plumbing out if we're having problems.

Margaret has gone to Mustique. Soon there will be nobody left.

'Bloody Sandringham!' she shouted as she kissed me goodbye, forgetting her cigarette-holder was still in her mouth.

19 January 1987   *Sandringham House*
Sarah, having learnt to fly light aircraft, is now going to have helicopter lessons; she seems to be determined that anything Andrew does, she can do better. I wonder if I could send her to the Falklands for a few months with the Navy . . . that would certainly stave off any latent Argentinian threat. She is such a bad influence on Diana, too. Last Sunday they were both giggling at the vicar, and roared when the people taking the offertory didn't know whether to pass the plate to me or not. I always see that an equerry puts some money in on my behalf.

9 February 1987   *Buckingham Palace*
Back to London as I have investitures tomorrow. Sarah came rushing in to Sandringham this morning with her 'Biggles' goggles on and offered to fly me back. 'We can always land in Hyde Park if I miss the Palace,' she screamed as I dodged her punch. I came on the train, although now that we do not have a special royal train, just a coach tagged on to the back of an Intercity, it is not quite the same. For one thing, the carriages in front are full of drunken commuters, and the ticket inspector told me I could not use my Super Saver before ten o'clock. But once I'd offered him an MBE and showed him my senior citizens' railcard he was quite amenable.

12 February 1987   *Buckingham Palace*
Princess Michael wants me to bid on her behalf for the
Duchess of Windsor's jewels.

'It vill look better if you buy zem, Elizabet,' she said.

'Why do you want them?' I asked, not at all sure that I
wished to be involved.

'Her *Royal Highness* and I had zo much in common,' she said
mournfully.

The children want to appear in a television programme
called *It's a Knockout*, to raise money for charity. I see no
objection, as long as Charles and Diana do not appear.

'It's just like charades, Mummy,' said Edward, so I shall
enjoy that.

10 June 1987   *Buckingham Palace*
Mrs Thatcher came to kiss hands on being appointed PM for a
third term in office.

'But the election isn't until *tomorrow*, Margaret,' I insisted.
She is too self-confident for her own good.

Had lunch with Anne. She asked if she could be made
Princess Royal. I was flabbergasted – but so pleased.

'Diana's Princess of Wales, and Sarah's Duchess of York,
and I'm just a plain old Princess,' she mumbled, 'and *they*
weren't even born royal.'

I have added her to the Birthday Honours list.

13 June 1987   *Buckingham Palace*
Trooped the Colour. I felt a little foolish sitting in the pram-
like carriage that Queen Victoria used to use, but at my age it
beats riding side-saddle for two hours.

15 June 1987   *Windsor Castle*
The Garter Ceremony at Windsor, and great fun to see my ex-
Prime Minister Mr Callaghan dressed up in a feathered hat.

'I feel like Margaret Thatcher,' he quipped. I wondered how
he knew.

The children are filming *It's a Knockout*.

16 June 1987   *Windsor Castle*

The first day of Ascot. Sarah and Diana have been behaving like a couple of schoolgirls, poking people with umbrellas. So undignified. This evening I saw the first sequences of the *It's a Knockout* programme. It made the antics at Ascot seem dignified. Only Anne remained cool, calm and collected.

'So *that's* why he left the bloody Marines,' sulked Philip, 'to dress up with a load of actors and make a fool of himself.'

I shall not allow such an event again, even if it is for charity. It was nothing at all like charades.

2 July 1987   *Buckingham Palace*

Diana is behaving very strangely. I caught her practising opening her eyes and mouth very widely in the mirror.

'What on earth are you doing?'

'I'm practising my "Fergie" face,' she said, giggling. She then shook my hand and I got an electric shock. 'Sarah taught me to do that.'

Charles fell off his horse, Pedro, at polo today. How could I ever abdicate?

Wore a very old suit and hat for today's engagements just to show that the monarchy is still reliable and dependable. At least *I* look reassuringly the same.

28 July 1987   *Buckingham Palace*

Held an investiture this morning and an audience with the PM tonight. I was going to ask Mrs Thatcher what I should do about my children. Charles and Diana seem to be growing apart, Sarah and Andrew have become the clowns of the family, and Edward has spent more than half a year not deciding what he wants to do with his life. Then I suddenly had second thoughts and decided she might not be the best person from whom to seek advice.

2 August 1987   *Balmoral Castle*

Decided to open the Sandringham Fruit Farm to the public. Apparently there's a lot of money to be made from people prepared to 'pick their own'. Sounds like a very easy way to boost the coffers, and the fruit is doing very well thanks to the manure from the racing stud next door.

One of my first customers, I gather, was the dear Duchess of Kent, who picked 30 pounds of blackberries for which I charged her 35p a pound. I suppose I should have given her a discount, but if you do it for one member of the family you have to do it for everyone. Any Tom, Dick or Harry can trace his lineage to show that he's related to us. Once Lillian Gish wrote to say that she is double seventh cousin three times removed to Diana; even Lord Lucan is a second cousin twice removed. He'd probably be after my blackberries if he wasn't in hiding.

No, I mustn't feel guilty about the Duchess. After all, she *has* got ten acres of her own at Anmer Hall. I'll have some blackberry seeds sent round for her.

3 September 1987　　　　　　　　*Balmoral Castle*
I'm very worried about Charles. He has been to stay here without Diana and the children and keeps taking himself off into the hills. I just pray that he's not writing another children's book. Sarah is churning them out almost at the rate of Barbara Cartland. The royal family must not become too commercialized.

I decided to confide in Mrs Thatcher, who was just slipping a few loose slates back into place on the roof.

'I want to do something about my children,' I shouted.

'I think you're a little too old to have any more, Ma'am,' she replied.

I knew she was the wrong person to ask.

4 September 1987　　　　　　　　*Balmoral Castle*
William and Harry came to see me with their nanny. I had hardly turned my back for a second when I discovered that William had stripped off half a wall of tartan wallpaper. What a blessing Queen Victoria kept so many spare rolls. Mrs Thatcher was able to repair the damage by teatime. I went to my room this evening and had a long chat with my dogs. They are the only creatures that I get any sense from these days, and

they have never been known to leak anything to the press.

'They leak on the bloody carpet though, Lilibet,' said Philip. He seems to swear more than ever nowadays.

P.O. BOX EIIR

THE MALL

LONDON SW1

Claire Rayner's Advisory Service
P.O. Box 125
Harrow
Middx.

1st October 1987

Dear Claire,

I felt that I had to write to you. I am at the end of my tether and need some advice, but because my face is rather well-known I have to keep my address a secret and have therefore used a box number.

I am a 61-year-old working wife with four grown-up children. My ~~eldest~~ daughter is marvellous. She's been through some difficult times, but has won through and now everyone adores her. She's even given up swearing in public. It's my three sons that are now giving me cause for concern.

My eldest, Charles, has been married for six years and seems to have hit a rocky patch. In fact he and his wife have been apart for six weeks. I'm sending them off on a short tour of Germany next month and am hoping that this will help them sort out their differences - but it's a big worry, all the same.

My second son, Andrew, has married beneath him. She's a nice enough girl, but does not always know how to behave in public. She tends to dig people in the ribs and poke them with umbrellas at the races - and her dress sense often leaves a lot to be desired, too. Now she's encouraging my son to build a nine-bedroom, mock-Tudor residence costing £5 million in Berkshire. She's even had a 'granny flat' designed for my eventual occupation, would you believe! But my son is signed up with the Royal Navy until 1991: how will he ever afford it on a sailor's salary?

My youngest son, Edward, poses another problem - although there is no girl on the horizon as yet. Or perhaps that is the worry. He gave up a perfectly good career in the Royal Marines last year, and since then has been idling his time away playing silly games and getting heavily involved with theatricals. Every time I see him nowadays he's wearing tights and a codpiece, and he bows to himself in every mirror he passes. He's living at home at the moment and has filled his room with sticks of Leichner, feathered hats and 'Phantom of the Opera' posters. Today when I went to speak to him he told me to go away as he was learning the script of 'Peter and the Wolf'. Fairy stories today - and who knows what tomorrow?

Yours anxiously,

WORRIED OF WINDSOR.

Daily Mirror
27/X/87

Dear Worried of Windsor,

WELL, lovey, what a right royal problem you seem to have, and yet I can't help thinking that you might just be to blame, my darling. Have you been the kind of mother that your children can look up to? Obviously, to judge from your notepaper, you have money. Have you perhaps been swanning around the world and leaving the kiddies in the charge of a nanny? This would be bound to make them grow up confused and irresponsible.

Leave your eldest son to sort out his own marriage problems, and don't let your daughter-in-law feel inferior or intimidated by you (after all, you're only her mother-in-law). Your middle son will have to put a stop to her 'dream home' as he will never get a mortgage on a house costing £5 million, so that will soon blow over, lovey.

As for your youngest son, Edward, he is just that – young. It inevitably takes kids time to find their feet and there's nothing you can do about it. Just in case he does have a little problem, I am sending you one of my lovely leaflets on personal relationships.

The best thing *you* can do is to get out and about a bit more. Join a pensioners' club, or take up a hobby.

And do stop worrying, darling. I'm sure *you* had the same sort of problems when you were young.

CLAIRE RAYNER

Dear Claire,

I HAVE an embarrassing problem with facial hair. I am a 16-year-old girl and already have a beard

28 October 1987   *Buckingham Palace*
I am sending Charles and Diana on a state visit to Germany,
which should stop any ugly rumours about their marriage. I
have told them firmly that they are to be seen together at all
times, hold hands as much as possible, and perhaps have one
public kiss on the tour. Charles is also going to start making
controversial comments about modern architecture, which will
certainly detract from their marriage problems. We also
wondered whether Diana should wear some really outrageous
clothes – that again would give the media something else to
harp on about.

'Why don't you go back to the Emanuels?' I suggested.

30 October 1987   *Buckingham Palace*
Received a letter from Neil Kinnock suggesting that the next
Labour Party conference might be held at Buckingham Palace,
which would save on MPs' expenses travelling to the coast,
and him the possible embarrassment of falling into the sea
again.

Showed the letter to Mrs Thatcher, who laughed. I don't
think I've seen her laugh before, not since Edward Heath lost
the Conservative Party leadership, anyway.

'No, Your Majesty, let them all go to sea,' she said.

3 December 1987   *Buckingham Palace*
While doing the despatch boxes this evening (in between
writing my Christmas cards before the threatened postal
strike: when will the Post Office remember that it handles the
Royal Mail?) I found a copy of *Woman's Own* left in a strategic
position by Mrs T. It cannot have been accidental. She never
does anything accidentally. You'd think she'd be too busy
preparing for Mr Gorbachev's visit to read magazines.

It was left open at a survey which claims that I earn £1,400
an hour, or £23 a minute, whereas Mrs T. earns £9 an hour,
which is 15p a minute. Even Terry Wogan earns £3 a minute,
apparently (that has been underlined in red). However, what I
get is peanuts compared to the income of Bill Cosby, Paul
McCartney, Joan Collins or Sylvester Stallone, the latter

earning a staggering £183 a minute! Not one of them carries the overheads that I do. Don't they realize what astronomical rates I have to pay on Sandringham and Balmoral, the wages for 600 members of the Royal Household, the rising cost of horse-feed, and the very high standards I have to maintain? I shall thank Mrs T. for the article at next week's audience and demand an increase in the Civil List in the 1988 budget, this year *above* the rate of inflation. She can stick that in her pipe and smoke it! (Or is it only the Labour Party that smokes pipes . . .?)

25 December 1987   *Windsor Castle*
Another Christmas over. The days of quiet Christmases are a distant memory now that William and Harry are running around and into everything. I so much enjoyed yesterday, watching them open their presents, but by the end of the party this evening I was beginning to feel very weary. Perhaps I'm getting too old for chasing up and down the Waterloo Chamber with a balloon between my knees, an orange under my chin and a paper crown on my head. Mummy dozed off through dinner, so we just took her hand out of the gravy boat and let her sleep on.

When she woke up she said, 'Well, just a small one, then.'

Played a lovely new game that Andrew and Sarah devised. It's called 'Twenty Things I Have Never Done', which was great fun to compile. Margaret refused to play. She says she has done everything.

I won the game by writing down 20 in less than a minute. We will all check our lists next Christmas to see if we have done any of them. What fun!

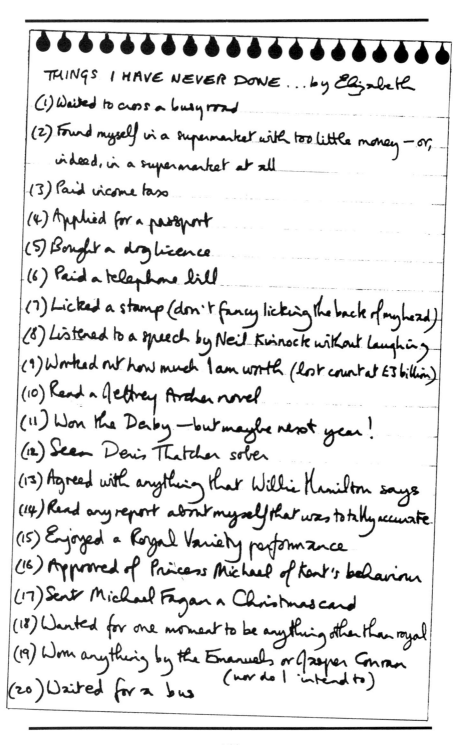

THINGS I HAVE NEVER DONE ... by Elizabeth

(1) Waited to cross a busy road

(2) Found myself in a supermarket with too little money — or, indeed, in a supermarket at all

(3) Paid income tax

(4) Applied for a passport

(5) Bought a dog licence

(6) Paid a telephone bill

(7) Licked a stamp (don't fancy licking the back of my head)

(8) Listened to a speech by Neil Kinnock without laughing

(9) Worked out how much I am worth (lost count at £3 billion)

(10) Read a Jeffrey Archer novel

(11) Won the Derby — but maybe next year!

(12) Seen Denis Thatcher sober

(13) Agreed with anything that Willie Hamilton says

(14) Read any report about myself that was totally accurate

(15) Enjoyed a Royal Variety performance

(16) Approved of Princess Michael of Kent's behaviour

(17) Sent Michael Fagan a Christmas card

(18) Wanted for one moment to be anything other than royal

(19) Worn anything by the Emanuels or Jasper Conran (nor do I intend to)

(20) Waited for a bus

1988

CRABTREE HALL
CLEGHORN ST PERCY
NORTH YORKSHIRE

3 January 1988

Your Majesty,

I do hope, Ma'am, that you will not mind my saying, as your confidante and friend, that your 1987 Christmas broadcast seemed a little dreary and unimaginative. May I be so bold as to suggest that you have a private word with our Oscar-winning film director Sir Richard Attenborough about making this annual event a little more lavish and exciting?

I would hate to presume upon his territory, but I must admit that after giving this some thought I have come up with a few ideas of my own, which I now humbly present below.

Christmas with the Royals!

1. MAIN TITLES
    Upbeat arrangement of the National Anthem sung by Shirley Bassey and Tom Jones. Shots of helicopter circling over London SW1 and homing in on Buckingham Palace.

    OPENING
    Camera pans across Buckingham Palace to reveal MEMBERS OF THE HOUSEHOLD hanging fairylights round the quadrangle, under supervision of MRS THATCHER.

    CUT TO -

2. THE GRAND STAIRCASE, Buckingham Palace
    A chorus line comprising the PRINCESS OF WALES, DUCHESS OF YORK, the PRINCESS ROYAL and PRINCESS MICHAEL OF KENT high-kicking down the stairs, followed by YOUR MAJESTY, smiling graciously and wearing red and white regalia, perhaps with the odd sprig of holly, as a nod in the direction of Father Christmas (marvellous imagery there, you see, of a benevolent and well-beloved monarch).
    When you reach the foot of the staircase, other MEMBERS OF THE ROYAL FAMILY join you for a verse or two of 'We Wish You a Merry Christmas'.

    CUT TO -

3. CLOSE-UP - HM QUEEN ELIZABETH II
    Into speech:

    At this festive time of year I would like you to join my family and me at our lovely London home. I would like to think that you are all here with me - in spirit if not in person.

/continued

Christmas is a time for being with our loved ones (CLOSE-UP of PRINCE PHILIP, pan across to the PRINCESS ROYAL) and our families (MEDIUM SHOT of whole ROYAL FAMILY); but it is also an occasion for looking with kindness upon those with whom we may not always see eye to eye (CLOSE-UP of PRINCESS MICHAEL, pan across to window to show MRS THATCHER decorating the Palace tree) and those who are less fortunate than ourselves (CLOSE-UP of MARK PHILLIPS). I think especially of the Commonwealth (CLOSE-UP of photo on piano of YOUR MAJESTY being lifted into the air on a barge in Tuvalu) and cherish warm memories of my friends in Northern Ireland (FILM of MR & MRS GERRY MURPHY of Ballybunion).

When Christ was born all those years ago, he came not to a palace, but to a stable (MEDIUM SHOT of the ROYAL MEWS); not for him the comforts of modern life (CLOSE-UP of Prince Philip's computer) but the straw used by oxen (CLOSE-UP of straw in Mews) and asses (CLOSE-UP of DENIS THATCHER helping MRS THATCHER down from the tree). Yet in 1988 I am glad to say that Christ is still here with us, in the comfort of our homes - in spirit, if not in person.

In 1988 my husband and I (CLOSE-UP of wedding photo) celebrated our Ruby Wedding anniversary (FILM of YOUR MAJESTY and PRINCE PHILIP at Luton Hoo, singing, 'We've Been Together Now for Forty Years...'); my daughter (CLOSE-UP of the PRINCESS ROYAL) celebrated fifteen years of marriage, and my son (CLOSE-UP of PRINCE ANDREW) reached his second anniversary (FILM of their party, with the DUCHESS OF YORK in her flying suit leaping out of a large iced cake). Yet at Christmas we all come together. Age and time cease to be important, and whether in a palace (MEDIUM SHOT of Buckingham Palace exterior) or a stable (LONG SHOT of Hampton Court Stud) we should never forget the true meaning of why we are here.

I think it was Shakespeare who said, 'If all the year were playing holidays, to sport would be as tedious as to work.' I hope that you will appreciate your holiday as much as we appreciate ours. (FILM of ROYAL FAMILY throwing snowballs at Sandringham.)

I wish you all a very happy Christmas, wherever you may be.

CUT TO -

4.   FINALE
The ROYAL FAMILY link arms (as in Sir Richard's lovely film A Chorus Line) and high-kick their way through a medley of Christmas songs (no doubt viewers at home will be thrilled to be able to singalongaroyal), followed by a firework display in front of Windsor Castle.

I am positive, Ma'am, that something along these lines would do much to boost your popularity in the TV ratings, and the show would certainly fill the gap left by Billy Smart's Circus in the Christmas Day schedules.

Your humble servant,

Constance, Lady Crabtree

10 January 1988   *Sandringham House*

Andrew is to be a father, which is very exciting but it came as something of a surprise as Sarah had said that she did not want children for a long time. It seems that they felt left out when they saw my 1987 Christmas card, which carried a photograph of Philip and me with our four grandchildren. So they decided to have a baby in time for this year's card.

Spoke to Mrs Thatcher on the telephone. She is very concerned that the House of Commons might be televised this year, and is trying desperately to keep the cameras out.

'Radio is one thing,' she said, 'but if I'm to be seen on television it will mean a new dress and a hair-do for each Prime Minister's Question Time.'

Personally I think she is more concerned that the public will *see* as well as hear her slaughtering Neil Kinnock each week. That could easily lead to a Labour victory – the British do so love the underdog.

15 February 1988   *Buckingham Palace*

Edward began work today as a production assistant for Andrew Lloyd Webber's Really Useful Theatre Company. He gets £180 a week for a nine-hour day, which is a nice little earner on top of his £20,000 a year from the Civil List. As yomping duties seem likely to be few and far between, he has been getting in some training by spending the last four weeks learning how to make a pot of tea. The Master of the Household has been showing him how to use tea bags, and actually took the trouble to buy a mug so that he could demonstrate how theatricals drink.

Just to show that he really does want to be treated as ordinary, Edward went to work with only a chauffeur and a detective – no police escort, personal valet, footman or anything. It is so kind of Mr Lloyd Webber to take on an inexperienced 23-year-old and give Edward a chance in life.

'Not had too strenuous a day lifting the teapot?' said Philip sarcastically when he returned. I do hope that one day he will forgive Edward for leaving the Marines and stop constructing assault courses in the corridor outside the boy's apartments.

16 February 1988   *Buckingham Palace*

Charles has made matters worse at home by sending Edward his recipe for nettle tea, which he thinks would be more beneficial to the Really Useful Company than PG Tips. Charles and Diana have a kitchenful of nettles at Highgrove, which I originally thought had been placed there to keep William and Harry out of the refrigerator.

'Where did we go wrong with our boys, Lilibet?' Philip asked sadly over supper this evening. 'Some people would give their eye-teeth to live in the comfort of a royal palace, yet there's Charles living in a barn in the middle of nowhere, talking to his stinging nettles; Andrew sits around all day while his wife flies helicopters and goes skiing even when she's pregnant, and Edward chooses the worst-paid job in the world's most overcrowded profession and ends up making the tea.'

Philip always gets maudlin when he sees people living the life he would secretly prefer.

'A stint in the forces, that's what they need,' he shouted. 'That would put hairs on their chests . . .'

I nodded in agreement. It's the only way when he's in one of those moods – no use at all pointing out that they've all been in the forces, and that could well be where the trouble started. He'll be 70 before we know it. Perhaps I can get him to retire, at least from being a patriarch.

18 March 1988   *Buckingham Palace*

Opened a new terminal at Gatwick Airport today. I opened the first in 1958, so it seemed only fair to go back. Decided not to make a speech (I hate having to wear my glasses in public) and limited the hand-shaking to fifteen people. I don't want to wear out like Philip.

I've been a little preoccupied with finances as the rates bill for Balmoral Castle arrived today. It has been slashed by £3 a year under the new Community Charge Plan for Scotland, but then the annual subscription to the Sandringham Women's Institute has gone up, so I don't gain a lot. I am more concerned with the new poll tax that my government wants to introduce. Buckingham Palace alone could cost me £40,000 a year as each of the resident staff will set me back £396. Cucumber sandwiches and cakes for the staff afternoon tea will have to end, and I shall begin charging Edward rent now that he's working full time. Must be careful how I handle him, though. When I suggested that Charles should lease his office from me, he moved it to St James's Palace. Could my properties be declared independent and exempt, I wonder . . .? As Queen I seem to be one of the few executives in the country with no perks.

How to pay the Poll Tax:

1.	Begin charging £10 a head at Palace garden parties	£240,000	a year
2.	Rent out the stables as luxury mews flats	£1,000,000	a year
3.	Charge rent on the 121 Grace and Favour apartments	£629,262.92	a year
	TOTAL	£1,869,262.92	

Looks like I could make quite a profit.

2 June 1988   *Windsor Castle*

The 35th anniversary of my Coronation. Philip gave me a lovely coral brooch – he's just a romantic old softie at heart, although he makes a good job of disguising it.

'Well, I suppose it's like a wedding anniversary,' he said. 'After all, you're married to the bloody job.'

'Only another 29 years to go and I will have beaten Queen Victoria,' I said comfortingly. 'I might consider abdicating then.'

'But I'll be 96!' he groaned.

'All right, I'll stay on an extra four years, then I can send you a telegram for your 100th birthday,' I reassured him. By the screams of delight he let out as he ran down the corridor, I knew he was thrilled with my decision.

Memo to self:
Consider Abdication
in AD 2021...

Epilogue

In the course of 35 years Her Majesty has made nearly 13,000 entries in her Journals, so this book contains a very small proportion of the total and the entries I have chosen were picked very much at random. Although politicians and presidents telephone me day and night to see what the Queen wrote on such-and-such a date, I feel it my duty to remain discreet regarding the other contents of the journals.

It was the great American statesman Adlai Stevenson who wrote that 'an editor is someone who separates the wheat from the chaff, and prints the chaff'. I hope that I have not selected too much chaff and that you will find many of the entries pure corn.

I do not yet know Her Majesty's views on the publication of her diaries, but I am positive she will be delighted.

GOD SAVE THE QUEEN!

> CONSTANCE, LADY CRABTREE
> Former Relief Woman of the Bedchamber to HM the Queen

10 DOWNING STREET
LONDON SW1A 2AA

14 September 1988

Your Majesty,

I was delighted to hear that you have released
your journals for publication - how very wise.
I think I might get Denis to leave a few volumes
of mine lying around the golf club just before the
next election.

I look forward to seeing you on Tuesday evening to
discuss the next Civil List increase.

Thank you so much for your salmon mousse recipe and
for the loan of the tiara.

As ever,

Margaret

The Rt. Hon. Mrs Margaret Thatcher PM

Her Majesty Queen Elizabeth II
Buckingham Palace
London SW1